Songs of

Independence

Songs of Independence

compiled and edited with historical notes by IRWIN SILBER

Stackpole Books

SONGS OF INDEPENDENCE

Copyright © 1973 by
Irwin Silber

Published by
STACKPOLE BOOKS
Cameron and Kelker Streets
Harrisburg, Pa. 17105

Printed in U.S.A.

Library of Congress Cataloging in Publication Data

Silber, Irwin, 1925-
    Songs of independence.

    With historical notes; includes songs and history
of the pre- and post- (1620-1812) American Revolutionary era.
    Bibliography: p.
    1. United States--History--Revolution--Songs and
music. 2. American ballads and songs. 3. English
ballads and songs.   I. Title.
M1631.S57S6   784.7'19'73   73-12323
ISBN 0-8117-1574-4

For Barbara Dane—
whose songs are for independence and revolution

Contents

CONTENTS

Acknowledgments

The author is indebted to several generations of historians, folklorists, antiquarians, researchers, journalists, and lovers of our Revolutionary tradition who have preserved the materials which have gone into the making of this work.

Many individuals have made contributions to this collection which have been acknowledged in the appropriate places. But the author would like particularly to thank four people who provided inestimable assistance. John Anthony Scott, whose own work in the area of Colonial and Revolutionary song and culture is widely known, provided invaluable help in locating many hard-to-find sources. John Allison made available to me his own creative and pioneering work in this field. Oscar Brand was, as always, both cooperative and generous in sharing his researches and thoughts with me. And Jerry Silverman brought his usual keen musical intelligence to the task of transcribing and re-creating the music in the form in which it appears here.

ACKNOWLEDGMENTS

Most of the research for this collection was done at the Library of Congress in Washington, D.C., where the staff of the Music Division and of the Folksong Archives helped in innumerable ways, and at the New York Public Library's Music, American History and Rare Book divisions, where an atmosphere of courtesy and concern always prevail.

The author's thanks to them all—not for himself alone, but on behalf of all those who may derive some enlightenment, enjoyment, or inspiration from this work.

Preface

This study of the songs associated with the development of American independence and political identity is, as will be readily apparent, at least as much sociological as it is musicological. But I have to confess that both of those sometimes awesome words are unsatisfactory, since they tend to categorize human activity by the way in which it is studied.

None of us live our lives solely, or even primarily, in those realms convenient to the disciplines of academia. Neither did the makers of the songs and ballads studied herein, nor the people the ballads are about.

The separation of art from other human activity, indeed the entire mystique imposed upon it, is particularly the outgrowth of our own historic epoch. The intensification of the historic divisions of labor by the advanced technological requirements of our age has tended to idolize—and thereby isolate—the individual gifted artist.

Fortunately, there are signs throughout the world that this separation between art and life is coming to an end, and that a more rational age is dawning.

The new liberty which is already on the horizon is, in one very important sense, an extension of the spirit of independence which was this nation's midwife. What I am saying, of course, is that ours is an age of revolutionary change with old systems, old values and, yes, old personalities, being swept away by the tide of history.

As the bicentennial of this nation's independence approaches, there will be a tendency to celebrate the occasion with nostalgic ritual. But approaching this 200th year since that most outrageous of documents—the Declaration of Independence—was proclaimed to an undoubtedly bemused world offers us the opportunity to go beyond the safe pieties. We can, if we will, make of this moment an opportunity to rediscover that still-latent American "genius" which, at the time of the Declaration, was as democratic a force as the world had ever known.

For myself, this study represents the conclusion of a period in my life which has been largely devoted to exploring our history through the songs and ballads which were sung in the very moments of the historical process. Coming to learn and love these songs, I have come to know more about myself as a human being and, recognizing the possible pretentiousness of it, as an American. I have not always been happy with what I found, for what American can be proud of that part of our history which is rooted in the extermination of the Indian peoples, or the horrors of slavery and its legacy of racism, or the rapaciousness of those who plundered the continent's material and human resources?

But there is another side to this America. I found it in the songs of black men and women resisting slavery, and young farm boys who marched off to death singing of old John Brown. I found it in the songs of dirt farmers and homesteaders who tried desperately to hack a living out of the land and learned that in order to suvive they had to fight not only the depradations of nature but the concentrated economic power of railroads, banks and monopolies. I found it in the songs of those who tried to make things better for themselves and others—sometimes through the ballot box, and sometimes, like the miners of Ludlow, Colorado in 1912, by picking up a gun to defend their own.

And in working on this study, I found it once again in the songs that young farm boys and ragged foot soldiers sang as they defeated the world's most powerful army in the days of '76, demonstrating beyond any shadow of a doubt, one trusts, that revolution is as American as cherry pie.

chapter I

The Roots of Independence

Songs of Rising American Consciousness, 1620-1763

"No government is to be submitted to at the *expence* of that which is the *sole end* of all government—the common good and safety of society." So spoke a Congregational minister by the name of Jonathan Mayhew in Boston in 1750, twenty-six years before the Declaration of Independence.

Where does American independence begin? Whatever date one chooses—1776, 1763, 1690, 1620—one may find evidence from an earlier time to demonstrate that the roots of an American nationality are as old as the first inhabitants of North America. For even before the age of "discovery," the peoples of this continent had evolved over the course of centuries a culture and a variety of forms of political organization based upon the particular natural and socially evolved environment of North America.

Starting points, therefore, are inevitably arbitrary—pinpoints of time imposed upon events which, in turn, have their origins in previous experience. Our starting point is the presence of Europeans on this continent—first as explorers, then as traders and entrepreneurs, then as colonizers and settlers, and finally as "native-born" Americans.

More than 150 years elapsed between the time of the first English settlement in North America at Jamestown, Virginia and that declaration of national independence which marks the birth of this nation. But it was in the interaction between the once European settler and a new set of social realities that independence was born. Although the term had not yet been invented, both John Smith of the Jamestown settlement and William Bradford of the Plymouth colony were "Americans." So, too, were the anonymous black men and women who arrived in Virginia in 1619 and became the first slaves on this continent.

Few, if any, conceived of themselves as "Americans," but the new consciousness emerging from their experience was lending shape and credence to a spirit—and ultimately political forms—that would, of necessity, be "independent" of the old world to the east which, then, seemed like the wellspring of their universe.

As the English settlements proliferated along the Atlantic coast, the territory which would, in time, become the first thirteen states of the American Union, appeared to be merely a British transplant. The clothing, the philosophy, the literature, the music—in short, the culture of these colonies—was outwardly English in almost all respects. But this outer appearance served to disguise something much more substantial which had begun to emerge: namely, concerns having more to do with the immediate realities of life in America than with an England two months plus a lifetime's journey away.

Even New England's stern God was a "God of my justice," a deity whose omniscience was of far greater consequence than the temporal pronouncements of kings—even English kings. And considering that God's appointed faithful in the New World had no need for the Church of England to interpret God's will for them, the very tenets of puritanism contained the seeds of independence.

Oxford[1]

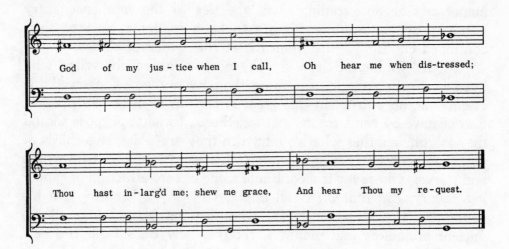

God of my jus-tice when I call, Oh hear me when dis-tressed;

Thou hast in-larg'd me; shew me grace, And hear Thou my re-quest.

Ye sons of men my glory turn
To shame, how long will you?
How long will ye love vanity
And still deceit pursue?

But know the Lord hath set apart
For him his gracious saint;
The Lord will hear when unto him
I pour out my complaint.

Be stirred up, but do not sin,
Consider seriously
Within your heart, with silence deep
When on your bed you lie.

The sacrifice of righteousness
Let sacrificed be;
And confidently put your trust
Upon the Lord, do ye.

But religion itself reflected a more material reality. To the privileged classes in North America—those with the closest commerical ties to Britain, the appointed officeholders, the military representatives—loyalty to England and a consciousness of being English were spiritual incarnations of those realities which defined their lives. But to the colonial farmer, the artisan, the smaller merchant and, in time, those who aspired to become the American manufacturing and trading class, the ties to the mother country began to appear more and more to be a matter subject to their continued choosing rather than the eternal order of things.

Michel-Guillaume Jean de Crevecoeur, a French writer who lived in North America for more than twenty years, assayed the essence of this spirit. "In this great American asylum, the poor of Europe have by some means met together.... to what purpose should they ask one another what countrymen they are? Alas, two thirds of them had no country. Can a wretch who wanders about, who works and starves, whose life is a continual scene of sore affliction or pinching penury; can that man call England or any other kingdom his country?... *He* is an American, who, leaving behind him all his ancient prejudices and manners, receives new ones from the new mode of life he has embraced...." Ironically, in later years, Crevecoeur discovered that he was not all that prepared for the political consequences of his cogent insights. When the Revolution finally came, Crevecoeur became a Loyalist.

But what the Frenchman expressed in a literary effusion typical of the day was being echoed, in its own way, in the penny broadsides sold in the London streets.

An Invitation To North America[2]

Come all you bold Brit-ons, wher-ev-er you be, I would have you draw near, and lis-ten to me. The times they get hard-er in Eng-land ev-'ry day, It is much bet-ter liv-ing in North A-mer-i-ca.

There is many a family of late that has gone
Away to New York, father, mother and son;
Let us likewise follow and make no delay,
For 'tis much cheaper living in North America.

The farmers in England sell their corn so dear,
They do what they can to starve the poor here.
They send it to France, which sure is not right,
To feed other nations that against us do fight.

Why do we stay here for to be their slaves,
When in Nova Scotia we can do as we please;
For who'd work in England for ten pence a day,
When we can get four shillings in North America.

The landlords in England do raise the lands high,
It forces some farmers abroad for to fly;
If times grow no better, I'll venture to say,
Poor men had better go to North America.

Observe then good people what to you I've told,
What a plague is in England by short weight of gold.
With bad silver and halfpence, believe what I say,
There's nothing of this in North America.

The priests in England come into the field,
They tithe as they please, you dare not but yield;
This is a great hardship, you believe, I dare say.
But we'll have no taxes in North America.

There's many a farmer you very well know,
That went to New York but a few years ago,
Have bought land and houses; who now would here stay—
But go and make fortunes in North America.

Manufactures in England are grown very bad,
For weavers and combers no work's to be had.
But let's go abroad, I dare venture to say,
They'll find us employment in North America.

So here's a health to George our gracious king,
I hope none will take amiss the song that I sing;
Then lads and lasses now come away,
And ship yourselves to North America.

Of course, that was only one side of the story. The other side had to do with tales of indentured servants and unwilling emigrants who found the work hard and the comforts few. But even these contributed to the growing awareness of an America that was somehow basically different from the mother country. In a street ballad entitled "A Net for a Night Raven; Or a Trap for a Scold," a cuckolded husband punishes his unfaithful wife by "selling" her for ten pounds to a sea captain bound for Virginia.

> . . . I know of women you are lacking,
> I now have one that I can spare,
> And her I can send packing.
> The times are very hard,
> I'll sell my wife for money,
> She is a proper handsome lass,
> And fitting for Virginny.

Another woeful ballad sounds as though the author had some experience with life in North America.

The Trappan'd Maiden (or The Distressed Damsel)[3]

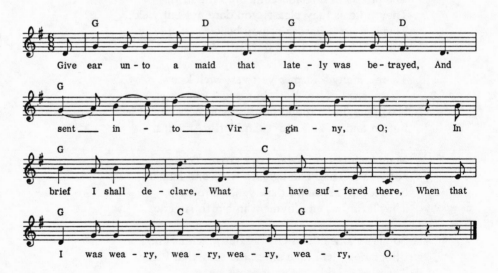

Give ear un-to a maid that late-ly was be-trayed, And sent___ in-to___ Vir - gin - ny, O; In brief I shall de-clare, What I have suf-fered there, When that I was wea-ry, wea-ry, wea-ry, wea-ry, O.

When that first I came
To this land of fame,
Which is called Virginny, O.
The axe and the hoe
Have brought my overthrow,
When that I was weary, etc.

Five years served I
Under Master Guy,
In the land of Virginny, O.
Which made me for to know
Sorrow, grief and woe,
When that I was weary, etc.

When my Dame says, "Go,"
Then I must do so,
In the land of Virginny, O.
When she sits at meat,
Then I have none to eat,
When that I was weary, etc.

The clothes that I brought in
They are worn very thin,
In the land of Virginny, O.
Which makes me for to say,
Alas and well-a-day,
When that I was weary, etc.

Instead of beds of ease,
To lie down when I please,
In the land of Virginny, O:
Upon a bed of straw,
I lay down full of woe,
When that I was weary, etc.

Then the spider she,
Daily waits on me,
In the land of Virginny, O;
Round about my bed
She spins her tender web,
When that I am weary, etc.

So soon as it is day,
To work I must away,
In the land of Virginny, O:
Then my dame she knocks
With her tinder-box,
When that I was weary, etc.

I have played my part,
Both at plow and cart,
In the land of Virginny, O:
Billets from the wood,
Upon my back they load,
When that I was weary, etc.

Instead of drinking beer,
I drink the water clear,
In the land of Virginny, O:
Which makes me pale and wan,
Do all that e'er I can,
When that I was weary, etc.

If my dame says, "Go!"
I dare not say no,
In the land of Virginny, O:
The water from the spring
Upon my head I bring,
When that I was weary, etc.

When the child doth cry,
I must sing, "By a by,"
In the land of Virginny, O.
No rest that I can have,
Whilst I am here a slave,
When that I was weary, etc.

A thousand woes beside,
That I do here abide,
In the land of Virginny, O:
In misery I spend
My time that hath no end,
When that I was weary, etc.

Then let maids beware,
All by my ill-fare,
In the land of Virginny, O:
Be sure you stay at home,
For if you do here come,
You all will be weary, etc.

But if it be my chance,
Homewards to advance,
From the land of Virginny, O:
If that I once more
Land on English shore,
I'll no more be weary,
weary, weary, weary, O.

America's traditional self-image as a land of unbridled opportunity, rich natural resources and just rewards for hard work and moral virtue has been perpetuated, in part, by songs such as "An Invitation to North America" and, in later years, The Hutchinson family's "Uncle Sam's Farm." But frequently, a more jaundiced view crept into the broadside ballads. The saga of what might be called "the disillusioned traveler" keeps cropping up from time to time. Here an anonymous English ballad-maker sometime around the turn of the eighteenth century dispels a few myths concerning North America.

A New England Ballad[4]

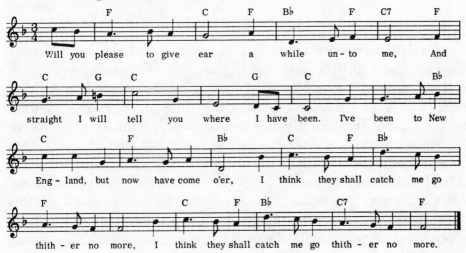

Will you please to give ear a while un-to me, And straight I will tell you where I have been. I've been to New Eng-land, but now have come o'er, I think they shall catch me go thith-er no more, I think they shall catch me go thith-er no more.

Before I went thither, Lord how folk did tell,
How wishes did grow and how birds did dwell,
All one 'mongst t'other in the wood and the water,
I thought that was true, but I found no such matter.

When first I did land, they 'mazed me quite,
And 'twas of all days on a Saturday night;
I wondered to see strange buildings were there,
'Twas all like the standings at Woodbury Fair.

Well, that night I slept till near prayer time,
Next morning I wondered I heard no bells chime;
At which I did ask and the reason I found,
'Twas because they had ne'er a bell in the town.

At last being warned, to church we repaired,
Where I did think certain we should have some prayers;
But the parson there no such matter did teach,
They scorned to pray for all one could preach.

The first thing they did, a psalm they did sing,
I plucked out my Psalm-book I with me did bring;
And tumbled to seek it, 'cause they called it by name,
But they'd got a new song to the tune of the same.

Now this was New Dorchester, as they told unto me,
A town very famous in all that country;
They said 'twas new buildings, I grant it is true,
Yet methinks Old Dorchester's as fine as the new.

Clashes between the colonial authorities and the settlers were endemic under British rule. With few exceptions, however—such as Bacon's Rebellion in Virginia in 1676, Leisler's Rebellion in New York in 1690 and the New England uprising of 1689—these antagonisms did not significantly threaten England's hold over her North American possessions. Still, before the year 1700, the Massachusetts General Court declared that "the lawes of England are bounded within the fower [four] seas and do not reach America"—a revolutionary thesis if there ever was one. Usually these clashes appeared as class rather than national conflicts, but since it was the colonial ruling class which most identified with the crown, an independence theme is implicit in all of these struggles.

As a case in point, the following ballad celebrates the freeing of a Yankee prisoner from a colonial jail in Massachusetts sometime in the period 1730-40. The John Webber of the song appears to have been a mint master near Salem during colonial days. His imprisonment was connected with the agitation in New England at the time because of changes in the currency regulations. The old currency, or tender, popularly known as "old tenor," was replaced with new, paper currency. Webber apparently objected to the move and presumably refused to handle the new currency, thus earning the sobriquet, "Old Tenor," for himself. When the mint master's friends concluded that he had been unjustly jailed, they decided to take matters into their own hands. The "Billy" of the song is evidently one of Webber's friends who helped engineer the escape.

The Escape of Old John Webber [5]

Smoothly (♩ = 144)

There were nine to guard the Brit - ish ranks, And five to guard the town a - bout, And two to stand at ei - ther hand, And one to let Old Ten - or out.

Chorus:

Bil - ly broke locks and Bil - ly broke bolts, And Bil - ly broke all that he came nigh, Un - til he came to the dun - geon door, And that he broke right man - ful - ly.

> They mounted their horse and away did ride
> (And who but they rode gallantly),
> Until they came to the river bank
> And there they alighted right merrily.
>
> And then they called for a room to dance
> (And who but they danced merrily),
> And the best dancer among them all
> Was old John Webber who was just set free. (Cho.)

"Sometimes heavy, half-witted men get a knack of Rhyming, but it is Time to break them of it when they grow Abusive, Insolent and Mischievous with it." So spoke James Delancey, chief justice of the Supreme Court of New York on October 15, 1734. The immediate cause of Delancey's wrath was "two Scandalous Songs that are handed about."

The songs in question had been published surreptitiously by John Peter Zenger, the editor and publisher of the *New York Weekly Journal*, who shortly thereafter was indicted for "libel" because his paper had exposed the malfeasance of Governor Cosby and others in his administration. But the songs themselves were the outgrowth of a political struggle that had rocked the colony for several months previous.

William Cosby was one of those typically autocratic royal governors who seem to be the inevitable by-products of colonial systems. The royal governors of the American Colonies were, at best, an unappetizing lot. More often than not, they were political appointees whose claim on office was based on little more than a blood relationship with someone currently in favor at the British court. Frequently, a post in the Colonies was used as a convenient device for removing politically embarrassing or singularly inept, albeit influential, figures from the English scene. Cosby seems to have been the prototype of the clan.

Surrounding himself with sycophants among the local merchants, and himself politically ambitious, Cosby managed to alienate most of the common people with his arbitrary and dictatorial methods. Zenger's *Journal*, secretly financed by several dissident lawyers, led the attack on Cosby. The focal point of the struggle became the elections to the Common Council in September of 1734. Up until that time, the popularly elected Council had been little more than a servile tool of the governor. The Popular Party, with its base largely among the local artisans and small merchants, was organized and fielded a slate of candidates to oppose the incumbents, all of whom (with one exception) had pledged their support to Cosby.

The election took place September 29, 1734 and resulted in an overwhelming defeat for the governor. Only one of his supporters won re-election and that contest, in the wealthiest ward of the city, was decided by one vote. All the other seats were won by the Popular Party. The people were jubilant, and their sense of triumph was underscored a few days later with the appearance of a printed broadside containing two songs celebrating the outcome of the election.

A Song Made Upon the Election of New Magistrates for This City[6]

Tune: "To You Fair Ladies Now on Land"[7]

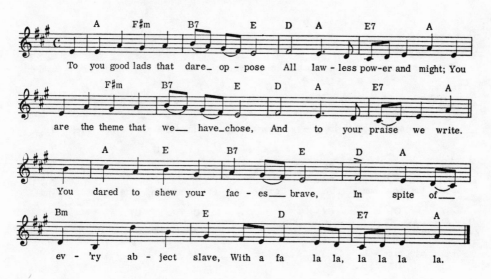

To you good lads that dare oppose All lawless power and might; You are the theme that we have chose, And to your praise we write. You dared to shew your faces brave, In spite of every abject slave, With a fa la la, la la la la.

Your votes you gave for those brave men
Who feasting did despise,
And never prostituted pen
To certify the lies
That were drawn up to put in chains,
As well our nymphs as happy swains,
   With a fa la la, la la la la.

And though the great ones frown at this,
What need have you to care?
Still let them fret and talk amiss,
You'll shew you boldly dare
Stand up to save your Country dear,
In spite of usquebaugh[8] and beer,
    With a fa la la, la la la la.

They begged and prayed for one year more,
But it was all in vain:
No wolawants[9] you'd have, you swore,
By Jove, you made it plain;
So sent them home to take their rest,
And here's a health unto the rest,
    With a fa la la, la la la la.

A Song Made Upon the Foregoing Occasion

Tune: "Now, Now You Tories All Shall Stoop" [10]

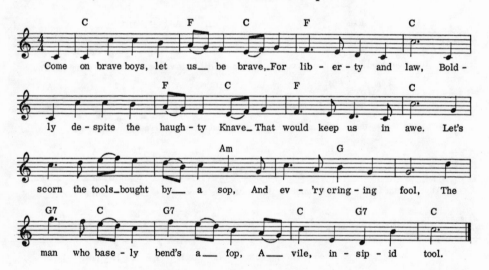

Our Country's Rights we will defend,
Like brave and honest men;
We voted right and there's an end,
And so we'll do again.
We vote all signers out of place,
As men who did amiss,
Who sold us by a false address,
I'm sure we're right in this.

Exchequer courts, as void by law,
Great grievances we call;
Though great men do assert no flaw
Is in them, they shall fall,
And be contemn'd by every man
That's fond of liberty;
Let them withhold it all they can,
Our Laws we will stand by.

Though pettyfogging knaves deny us
Rights of Englishmen,
We'll make the scoundrel rascals fly,
And ne'er return again.
Our judges they would chop and change
For those that serve their turn,
And will not surely think it strange
If they for this should mourn.

Come fill a bumper, fill it up,
Unto our Aldermen;
For Common-Council fill the cup,
And take it o'er again.
While they with us resolve to stand
For liberty and law,
We'll drink their healths with hat in hand
Whoraa! Whoraa! Whoraa!

Some particulars of these two songs deserve comment. First, of course, is the reference in both to "Country"—clearly an expression of at least the germ of Independence, although most colonists at the time would have viewed England as their "country." Still, when one defends "Our Country's Rights," clearly these are being opposed by some alien force.

More specifically, the phrase "who feasting did despise" in the first song refers to a "loyalty" banquet given by Governor Cosby in June of 1734, at which time he elicited expressions of loyalty (the "false address" of the second song) from members of the Council. Presumably "usquebaugh" was served on the occasion. Cosby was apparently the "haughty Knave," while exchequer courts were special bodies whose purpose was to collect taxes for the crown.

While no author is credited with the songs, the general suspicion—well-founded to be sure—was that they were the work of James

Alexander, a Colonial lawyer and one of the secret subsidizers of Zenger's paper.

A more experienced governor than Cosby might have gotten the message from the election and the songs and set to work to mend his political fences. But it was the age of "divine right," aristocracy and autocracy. Cosby was enraged at what he considered an affront to himself personally and a grave threat to the stability of British rule. A grand jury was impaneled and after having viewed the offending songs—we presume that the laws of evidence did not require their performance—concluded that they were

> both highly defaming the present Administration of His Majesty's Government in this Province, tending greatly to inflame the minds of His Majesty's good Subjects, and to disturb and destroy that Peace and Tranquility which aught to subsist and be maintained in this Colony and in all other well-governed Communites. . . .

However, since they could not discover the authors or publishers of the offending rhymes, the grand jury ordered that

> said Virulent, Scandalous and Seditious Songs or Ballads be burnt before the City Hall . . . by the hands of the Common Hangman or Whipper, on Monday, the 21st of this Instant, at 12 o'clock, and that the High Sheriff of this City and County do take order accordingly.

Cosby himself went on to offer a reward of twenty pounds for information leading to the conviction of the authors of the songs, but to no avail. But the burning of the songs hardly ended matters. As if to plague the governor to death with rhymes, a new crop of broadsides appeared, among them "a mournful Elegy on the Funeral pile and Execution of a ballad or ballads burnt by publick authority before a great small town in a certain country under the Northern Hemisphere [on a] certain day since the year 1600."

Another, "The Last Words and Testament of the Song on the Election," may have helped Cosby realize—as other rulers have in time—that "banning" a work is about the least effective method for dealing with its ideas. Its conclusion can well serve as our last word on the matter.

By impious hands to flames condemed,
Because in tuneful ways,
The generous patriots fame I sang,
And the base fops dispraised.

In time, overtones of independence could be heard in the class struggles of the gradually stratifying colonial society. The responsibility of the crown for maintaining law and order and the view of the British empire-builders that the Colonies were little more than exploitable territories helped translate underlying economic rivalries into political conflict.

But there were many factors working to reinforce the relationship between the Colonies and England. Chief among these, perhaps, was the presence and continuing threat of enemies—specifically the French and the dispossessed Indians. For more than half a century, both the British and the French had tried to develop alliances with the Indian nations. But as it became clear that it was the English who were expropriating the land at the most rapid pace, the Indians threw their lot in with the French.

These conflicts culminated in the Seven Years War (1756-1763), fought by the British and the American colonists against the French and the Indians. To the Europeans, the North American conflict was only one front in the (to them) far more decisive struggle raging on the continent.

But while the threat of a common foe kept the settlers and the mother country united, it was this struggle which became the immediate precipitating cause of the Revolution itself. First, the colonial assemblies, who had been chipping away at the prerogatives of the crown for many decades, utilized Britain's critical position during the war to wrest concessions in terms of self-rule and local autonomy which served to extend self-government to a point of almost no return. Second, the defeat of the French reduced the Colonies' reliance on England. And lastly, the vast expenditures of the war—in Europe as well as North America—forced the British to turn to the Colonies, beinning in 1763, as a new and significant source of revenue. The hated Sugar Act and Stamp Act of the immediate postwar period resulted, with the attendant leap in colonial resistance and the serious beginning of an independence movement.

As they did for a hundred years before and more than that afterwards, the British fought the Seven Years War in North America with not only their own young men, but even more with Irish recruits. The songs of these unwilling Irish soldiers over the span of Britain's imperial wars would fill a small volume by themselves. Here is one that has survived in the folk memory from the days of the North American war.

Felix the Soldier [11]

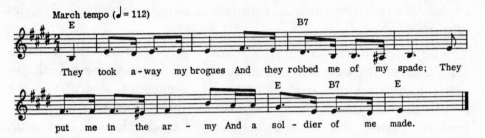

March tempo ($\quad$ = 112)

They took a-way my brogues And they robbed me of my spade; They put me in the ar - my And a sol - dier of me made.

But I couldn't beat the drum,
And I couldn't play the flute,
So they handed me a musket
And taught me how to shoot.

We had a bloody fight
After we had scaled the wall,
And the divil a bit of mercy
Did the Frenchies have at all.

But the Injuns they were sly,
And the Frenchies they were coy,
So they shot off the left leg
Of this poor Irish boy.

Then they put me on a ship
And they sent me home again,
With all my army training
After battle's strife and din.

I will bid my spade adieu,
For I cannot dig the bog,
But I still can play a fiddle
And I still can drink my grog.

I have learned to smoke a pipe
And have learned to fire a gun,
To the divil with the fighting,
I am glad the war is done.

The decisive battle of the French and Indian War was the capture of Quebec in 1759 by a British army under the command of General James Wolfe. With a distinguished military record earned from earlier fights, Wolfe grew into a legendary figure following his death on the battlefield during the capture of Quebec. For many years the ballad of the death of General Wolfe was sung throughout the North American continent with the same respect accorded the old British ballads brought here with the first settlers. And in sections of British Canada and northern New York State today, one can still come upon an old ballad singer who will recount the sad tale of "Brave Wolfe."

Brave Wolfe [12]

I went to see my love only to woo her,
I went to gain her love, not to undo her;
Whene'er I spake a word my tongue did quiver,
I could not speak my mind while I was with her.

Love, here's a diamond ring, long time I've kept it,
'Tis for your sake alone, if you'll accept it.
When you the posy read, think on the giver,
Madam, remember me, or I'm undone forever.

Brave Wolfe then took his leave of his dear jewel,
Most sorely did she grieve, saying, "Don't be cruel."
Said he, "tis for a space that I must leave you,
Yet love, where'er I go, I'll not forget you."

So then this gallant youth did cross the ocean,
To free America from her commotion.
He landed at Quebec with all his party,
The city to attack both brave and hearty.

Brave Wolfe drew up his men in form most pretty,
On the Plains of Abraham, before the city;
There just before the town the French did meet them,
With double numbers they resolved to beat them.

When drawn up in a line, for death prepared,
While in each others face their armies stared;
So pleasantly brave Wolfe and Montcalm talked,
So martially between their armies walked.

Each man then took his post at their retire,
So then these numerous hosts began to fire;
The cannon on each side did roar like thunder,
And youths in all their pride were torn asunder.

The drums did loudly beat, colours were flying,
The purple gore did stream and men lay dying;
When shot from off his horse fell this brave hero,
And we lament his loss in weeds of sorrow.

The French began to break their ranks and flying,
Brave Wolfe then seemed to wake as he lay dying,
He lifted up his head while guns did rattle,
And to his army said, "How goes the battle?"

His aide-de-camp replied, "'Tis in our favor,
Quebec with all her pride, we soon shall have her;
She'll fall into our hands with all her treasure."
"Oh, then," replied brave Wolfe, "I die with pleasure."

chapter II

Songs of the Revolutionary Agitation

From Protest
to Armed Resistance, 1763-1775

While the spirit of independence grew slowly in the North American colonies for a century and a half, with the conclusion of the French and Indian War, the notion suddenly came to life. It is no coincidence that the period of revolutionary agitation commences in 1763 with the formal end of hostilities between the British and the French.

During the war, England had acquired a new king—George III, who succeeded to the throne in 1760. But it was another George, Chancellor of the Exchequer George Grenville, who did more than any other man to bring on the American Revolution. Rising to the treasury post in 1763, he immediately undertook a series of revenue-raising acts aimed at producing an income for the mother country out of taxes to be imposed on the Colonies. Chief among these were taxes on sugar and the notorious Stamp Tax, which imposed a levy on all printed documents. Grenville accompanied his revenue meas-

35

ures with a series of regulations concerning their collection which soon became even more odious to colonial merchants than the taxes themselves.

But it wasn't the merchants alone who chafed under the new duties. Increased costs were, naturally, passed along to the consumer. The crack-down on violations soon involved tens of thousands, many of whom lived by smuggling of a sort. As the result of arbitrary seizures and arrests, trials in distant locations and the whole panoply of law by fiat of British officials, a wave of resentment swept the Colonies. This situation produced what may well be considered the opening anthem of the revolution, a ballad composed by a Norwalk, Connecticut school teacher, Peter St. John, in the year 1765.

American Taxation [1]

Words: Peter St. John
Tune: "The British Grenadiers"

> While I relate my story, Americans give ear;
> Of Britain's fading glory, you presently shall hear.
> I'll give a true relation, attend to what I say,
> Concerning the taxation of North America.
>
> The cruel lords of Britain, who glory in their shame,
> The project they have hit on they joyfully proclaim;
> 'Tis what they're striving after our rights to take away,
> And rob us of our charter in North America.
>
> There are two mighty speakers who rule in Parliament,
> Who ever have been seeking some mischief to invent;
> 'Twas North,[2] and Bute[3] his father, the horrid plan did lay,
> A mighty tax to gather in North America.
>
> [North and Bute enlist the help of Satan in their diabolic
> plot to "subdue without resistance this North America." Then ...]
>
> These subtle arch-combiners addressed the British court,
> All three were undersigners of this obscure report—
> There is a pleasant landscape that lieth far away,
> Beyond the wide Atlantic in North America.

There is a wealthy people who sojourn in that land,
Their churches all with steeples most delicately stand;
Their houses like the gilly, are painted red and gay:
They flourish like the lily in North America.

Their land with milk and honey continually doth flow,
The want of food or money they seldom ever know:
They heap up golden treasure, they have no debts to pay,
They spend their time in pleasure in North America.

O King, you've heard the sequel of what we now subscribe,
Is it not just and equal to tax this wealthy tribe?
The question being asked, his majesty did say,
My subjects shall be taxed in North America.

Invested with a warrant, my publicans shall go,
The tenth of all their current they surely shall bestow;
If they indulge rebellion, or from my precepts stray,
I'll send my war battalion to North America.

I'll rally all my forces by water and by land,
My light dragoons and horses shall go at my command;
I'll burn both town and city, with smoke becloud the day,
I'll show no human pity for North America.

My gallant ships are ready to waft you o'er the flood,
And in my cause be steady, which is supremely good;
Go ravage, steal and plunder, and you shall have the prey;
They quickly will knock under in North America.

The laws I have enacted, I never will revoke,
Although they are neglected my fury to provoke.
I will forbear to flatter, I'll rule the mighty sway,
I'll take away the charter from North America.

O George! you are distracted, you'll by experience find
The laws you have enacted are of the blackest kind.
I'll make a short digression, and tell you by the way,
We fear not your oppression in North America.

Our fathers were distresséd, while in their native land,
By tyrants were oppresséd, as we do understand;
For freedom and religion they were resolved to stray,
And trace the desert regions of North America.

> We are their bold descendants, for liberty we'll fight,
> The claim to independence we challenge as our right;
> 'Tis what kind Heaven gave us, who can it take away—
> O, Heaven sure will save us in North America.

St. John's verses were heady stuff indeed in 1765, but some among the colonists were already going beyond treasonous rhetoric to direct action. The Sons of Liberty had been organized in the same year with the express purpose of making the Stamp Act unworkable; their activities included ransacking admiralty offices, burning revenue records and the like.

As the conflict between the Colonists and the crown intensified, the rebellious Americans employed a variety of tactics. In 1768, Boston militants hit on the idea of a boycott of British goods—particularly those on which a tax had been imposed. British cloth was a special target and it became fashionable for young women to forswear English fashions and "to show clothes of your own make and spinning." It is estimated that British exports to the Colonies dropped by more than $3 million from 1768 to 1769.

To The Ladies [4]

Young la-dies in town, and those that live round, Wear none but your own coun-try lin-en; Of e-con-o-my boast, let your pride be the most To show clothes of your own make and spin-ning. What if home-spun, they say, be not quite so gay As bro-cades, be not in a pas-sion; For once it is known, 'tis much worn in town, One and all will cry out, 'tis the fash-ion!

And, as one, all agree, that you'll not married be
To such as will wear London factory,
But at first sight refuse, tell 'em such you will choose
As encourage our own manufactory.

No more ribbons wear, nor in rick silks appear,
Love your country much better than fine things;
Begin without passion, 'twill soon be the fashion
To grace your smooth locks with a twine string.

These do without fear, and to all you'll appear,
Fair, charming, true, lovely and clever;
Though the times remain darkish, young men may be sparkish,
And love you much stronger than ever.

Then make yourselves easy, for no one will tease ye
Nor *tax* you, if chancing to sneer
At the sense-ridden tools, who think us all fools;
But they'll find the reverse far and near.

While the conflict between the colonists and the mother country polarized, many on both sides of the Atlantic found it hard to believe that a "union" seen as so self-evidently "desirable" would readily be severed. One anonymous English parodist wrote a ditty which he called "The World Turned Upside Down or, The Old Woman Taught Wisdom." As a political allegory it clearly left much to be desired, but as an attempt to minimize the conflict and to at least suggest a somewhat even-handed view of events, it remains an interesting memento of the pre-Revolutionary period.

The Old Woman Taught Wisdom [5]

Words: Anonymous
Tune: "Derry Down"

Goody Bull and her daughter together fell out,
Both squabbled and wrangled and made a damned rout,
But the cause of the quarrel remains to be told,
Then lend both your ears and a tale I'll unfold.

The old lady, it seems, took a freak in her head,
That her daughter, grown woman, might earn her own bread:
Self-applauding her scheme, she was ready to dance;
But we're often too sanguine in what we advance.

For mark the event; thus by fortune we're crossed,
Nor should people reckon without their good host;
The daughter was sulky, and wouldn't come to,
And pray, what in this case, could the old woman do?

In vain did the matron hold forth in the cause,
That the young one was able; her duty, the laws;
Ingratitude vile, disobedience far worse;
But she might e'en as well sung psalms to a horse.

Young, forward and sullen, and vain of her beauty,
She tartly replied that she knew well her duty,
That other folks' children were kept by their friends,
And that some folks loved people but for their own ends.

Be damned! says the farmer, to the old woman he goes,
First roars in her ears, then tweaks her old nose,
Hallo Goody, what ails you? Wake! woman, I say;
I am come to make peace in this desperate fray.

Adzooks, ope thine eyes, what a pother is here!
You've no right to compel her, you have not, I swear;
Be ruled by your friends, kneel down and ask pardon,
You'd be sorry, I'm sure, should she walk Covent Garden.

Unwillingly awkward, the mother knelt down,
While the absolute farmer went on with a frown,
Come, kiss the poor child, there come, kiss and be friends!
There, kiss your poor daughter, and make her amends.

No thanks to you, mother, the daughter replied:
But thanks to my friend here, I've humbled your pride;
Then pray leave off this nonsense, 'tis all a mere farce,
As I have carried by point, you may now kiss my arse.

It is an interesting comment on the moral values of the times to realize that a young woman's "independence" was assumed to be the equivalent of "a life of shame" since "walking Covent Garden" was the way the London prostitutes advertised their wares.

But while some were trying to find a way to make peace through compromise, an adamant British ruling class and an increasingly radicalized band of American rebels were having at each other with a will. Newspapers, pamphlets, sermons and ballads became artful polemics in the heated struggle to direct the colonial consciousness. Of all the songs employed in this cause during the period, none was more popular than John Dickinson's "Liberty Song." Written in 1768 to the tune of "Hearts of Oak," it swept the Colonies and proved so effective that Tory songwriters felt obliged to respond with parodies.

The song itself was only one of several constructed along similar lines. The original "Hearts of Oak" was written in London in 1759 as a triumphant paean to British military successes in Africa, Europe and North America. With words by David Garrick and music by William Boyce, the song was a patriotic salute to the British Navy and its seamen. One verse of the original went:

Come cheer up, my lads, 'tis to glory we steer,
To add something more to this wonderful year:
To honor we call you, not press you like slaves,
For who are so free as the sons of the waves?
     Hearts of oak are our ships,
     Gallant tars are our men,
     We always are ready,
     Steady, boys, steady.

The song was popular, too, in the Colonies, and naturally lent itself to parodying in the developing antagonisms with England. The first such parody for which there is a record was fairly mild, demanding no more than the rights of Englishmen and affirming loyalty to the crown. But the seeds of subversion were to be found between the lines.

41

Hearts Of Oak Are We Still [6]

Tune: "Hearts of Oak"

Sure never was picture drawn more to the life,
Or affectionate husband more fond of his wife,
Than America copies and loves Britain's sons,
Who conscious of freedom, are bold as great guns.
    Hearts of oak are we still,
    For we're sons of those men,
    Who always are ready,
    Steady, boys, steady,
    To fight for their freedom
    Again and again.

Though we feast and grow fat on America's soil,
Yet we own ourselves subjects of Britain's fair isle,
And who's so absurd to deny us the name?
Since true British blood flows in every vein.
    Hearts of oak, etc.

Then cheer up my lads, to your country be firm,
Like kings of the ocean we'll weather each storm,
Integrity calls out, fair liberty, see,
Waves her flag o'er our heads and her words are: "Be free!"
    Hearts of oak, etc.

To King George, as true subjects, we loyal bow down,
But hope we may call Magna Charta our own.
Let the rest of the world slavish worship decree,
Great Britain has ordered her sons to be free.
    Hearts of oak, etc.

On our brow while we laurel-crowned Liberty wear,
What Englishmen ought, we Americans dare;
Though tempests and terrors around us we see,
Bribes nor fears can prevail o'er the hearts that are free.
    Hearts of oak, etc.

With Loyalty, Liberty let us entwine,
Our blood shall for both flow as free as our wine;
Let us set an example, what all men should be,
And a Toast give the world—"Here's to those who'd be free."
    Hearts of oak, etc.

Where the above only hinted at some of the underlying antagonisms between colony and crown, John Dickinson's "Liberty Song," written two years later and in the same mode, was an impassioned plea for the redress of wrongs. Dickinson himself was far from being an advocate of independence. In fact, as a delegate to the Continental Congress in 1776, he voted against the Declaration of Independence, although he subsequently served in the Revolutionary Army.

Given Dickinsons's moderate—if not conservative—political views, his "Liberty Song" becomes even more remarkable a reflection of the growing chasm between England and the Colonies. And yet, the song is cautious. It calls on Americans to give their money, not their lives, for "Liberty," not independence and separation. After writing the song early in 1768, Dickinson sent it off to James Otis of Massachusetts, the foremost spokesman among the anticrown "moderates" in the Bay Colony, with the following note:

> I enclose you a song for American freedom. I have long since renounced poetry, but as indifferent songs are very powerful on certain occasions, I venture to invoke the deserted muses. I hope my good intentions will procure pardon, with those I wish to please, for the boldness of my numbers. My worthy friend, Dr. Arthur Lee, a gentleman of distinguished family, abilities and patriotism, in Virginia, composed eight lines of it. Cardinal de Retz always enforced his political operations by songs. I wish our attempt may be useful.

An interesting sidelight on Dickinson's political caution is provided by a second letter to Otis, written two days after the first—

> I enclosed you the other day a copy of a song composed in great haste. I think it was rather too bold. I now send a corrected copy which I like better. If you think the bagatelle may be worth publishing, I beg it may be this copy. If the first is published before this is come to hand, I shall be much obliged to you if you will be so good as to publish this with some little note, "that this is the true copy of the original."

The evidence points to Otis having made the amendments in time since there is no record of a second version appearing in print— leaving us to speculate on what rash sentiments Dickinson expressed in the heat of political passion. We do know that the fifth verse— beginning "How sweet are the labors"—was an afterthought to the original, probably more the result of subsequent poetic inspiration than political modification. As to Arthur Lee, credited by Dickinson with having contributed eight lines, he was the youngest son of the distinguished Virginia family whose varied contributions to the Revolutionary cause would take several volumes to enumerate.

The Liberty Song [7]

Words: John Dickinson
Tune: "Hearts of Oak"

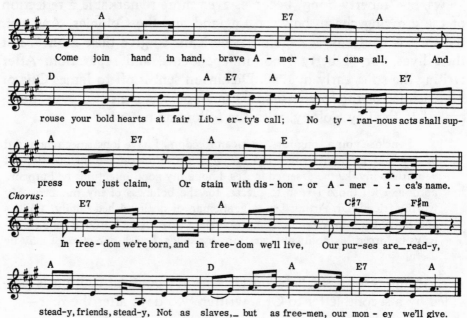

Come join hand in hand, brave A - mer - i - cans all, And rouse your bold hearts at fair Lib - er- ty's call; No ty - ran-nous acts shall sup- press your just claim, Or stain with dis - hon - or A - mer - i - ca's name.

Chorus:
In free - dom we're born, and in free-dom we'll live, Our pur-ses are—read-y, stead-y, friends, stead-y, Not as slaves,— but as free-men, our mon - ey we'll give.

Our worthy forefathers—let's give them a cheer—
To climates unknown did courageously steer;
Through oceans to deserts, for freedom they came,
And dying, bequeathed us their freedom and fame.

Their generous bosoms all dangers despised,
So highly, so wisely, their birthrights they prized;
We'll keep what they gave, we will piously keep,
Nor frustrate their toils on the land or the deep.

The Tree their own hands had to Liberty reared,
They lived to behold growing strong and revered;
With transport they cried—"Now our wishes we gain,
For our children shall gather the fruits of our pain."

How sweet are the labors that freemen endure,
That they shall enjoy all the profit, secure—
No more such sweet labors Americans know,
If Britons shall reap what Americans sow.

Swarms of placemen and pensioners soon will appear,
Like locusts deforming the charms of the year:
Suns vainly will rise, showers vainly descend,
If we are to drudge for what others shall spend.

Then join hand in hand brave Americans all,
By uniting we stand, by dividing we fall;
In so righteous a cause let us hope to succeed,
For Heaven approves of each generous deed.

All ages shall speak with amaze and applause,
Of the courage we'll show in support of our laws;
To die we can bear—but to serve we disdain,
For shame is to freemen more dreadful than pain.

This bumper I crown for our sovereign's health,
And this for Britannia's glory and wealth;
That wealth and that glory immortal may be,
If she is but just and we are but free.

A Loyalist response was not long in coming. The following "Parody Upon a Well-known Liberty Song" appeared in the pages of the *Boston Gazette*, September 26, 1768.

Parody Upon A Well-Known Liberty Song [8]

Words: Anonymous
Tune: "Hearts of Oak"

Come shake your dull noddles, ye pumpkins, and bawl,
And own that you're mad at fair Liberty's call;
No scandalous conduct can add to your shame,
Condemned to dishonor, inherit the fame.
    In folly you're born, and in folly you'll live,
    To madness still ready, and stupidly steady,
    Not as men but as monkeys the tokens you give.

Your grandsire, old Satan, now give him a cheer,
Would act like yourselves, and as wildly would steer:
So great an example in prospect still keep,
Whilst you are alive, Old Belza may sleep.

Such villains, such rascals, all dangers despise,
And stick not at mobbing when mischief's the prize;
They burst through all barriers, and piously keep
Such chattels and goods the vile rascals can sweep.

The Tree, which the wisdom of justice hath reared,
Should be stout for their use, and by no means be spared:
When fuddled with rum the mad sots to restrain,
Sure Tyburn will sober the wretches again.

Your brats and your bunters by no means forget,
But feather your nests, for they're bare enough yet;
From the insolent rich sure the poor knave may steal,
Who ne'er in his life knew the scent of a meal.

Then plunder, my lads, for when red coats appear,
You'll melt like the locust when winter is near;
Gold vainly will glow, silver vainly will shine,
But, faith you must skulk, you no more shall purloin.

Then nod your poor numskulls, ye pumpkins, and bawl,
The de'il take such rascals, fools, whoresons and all;
Your cursed old trade of purloining must cease,
The dread and the curse of all order and peace.

All ages shall speak with contempt and amaze,
Of the vilest banditti that swarmed in these days;
In defiance of halters, of whips and of chains,
The rogues would run riot—fools for their pains.

Gulp down your last dram, for the gallows now groans,
And, over depressed, her lost empire bemoans;
While we quite transported and happy shall be,
From mobs, knaves and villains, protected and free.

The Tory parody drew a sharp rejoinder from Colonial ranks. An examination of this whole series of parodies might well provide a textbook lesson in the ways of revolutionary escalation, for even this "parody parodized," published in November of 1768, is a far more militant call than the Dickinson song of four months earlier.

The Massachusetts Liberty Song [9]

Words: Anonymous
Tune: "Hearts of Oak"

Come swallow your bumpers, ye tories, and roar,
That the sons of fair Freedom are hampered once more;
But know that no cut-throats our spirits can tame,
Nor a host of oppressors shall smother the flame.
    In freedom we're born and like sons of the brave,
    We'll never surrender, but swear to defend her,
    And scorn to survive if unable to save.

Our grandsires, blest heroes, we'll give them a tear,
Nor sully their honors by stooping to fear;
Through deaths and through dangers, their trophies they won,
Who dare be their rivals, nor will be outdone.

Let tyrants and minions presume to despise,
Encroach on our rights and make freedom their prize:
The fruits of their rapine they never shall keep;
Though vengeance may nod, yet how short is her sleep!

Our wives and our babes, still protected, shall know,
Those who dare to be free, shall for ever be so;
On these arms and these hearts they may safely rely,
For in freedom we'll live, or like heroes we'll die.

Ye insolent tyrants! who wish to enthrall,
Ye minions, ye placemen, pimps, pensioners all,
How short is your triumph! how feeble your thrust!
Your honors must wither and nod to the dust.

When oppressed and reproached, our king we implore,
Still firmly persuaded our rights he'll restore;
When our hearts beat to arms, to defend a just right,
Our monarch rules there, and forbids us to fight.

Not the glitter of arms, nor the dread of a fray,
Could make us submit to their chains for a day;
Withheld by affection, on Britons we call—
Prevent the fierce conflict which threatens your fall!

All ages shall speak, with amaze and applause,
Of the prudence we show in support of our cause;
Assured of our safety, a Brunswick still reigns,
Whose free loyal subjects are strangers to chains.

> Then join hand in hand, brave Americans all!
> To be free is to live, to be slaves is to fall;
> Has the land such a dastard, as scorns not a lord,
> Who dreads not a fetter much more than a sword.

While the "ballad wars" of newspaper and penny broadside waxed hot during this period, the growing sense of revolutionary purpose went beyond what later generations would call "agit-prop" (from "agitational propaganda") songs. The first American composers begin to appear during this time. For many of them, "independence" meant the charting of a new musical course, the breaking of traditional modes of song and composition.

Probably the best-known of these was William Billings, a self-taught musician, a tanner by trade and an ardent patriot. In 1770, at the age of twenty-four, he produced his first work, a collection of his compositions gathered together under the general heading of *The New England Psalm Singer*. The temper of the man may be gathered from his foreword to this volume:

> Perhaps it may be expected by some, that I could say something concerning rules for composition; to these I answer that *Nature is the best Dictator*, for all the hard dry studied rules that ever were prescribed will not enable any person to form an Air any more than the bare knowledge of the four and twenty letters, and strict Grammatical rules will qualify a scholar for composing a piece of poetry. . . . It must be Nature; Nature must lay the Foundation, Nature must give the Thought. . . .

> For my own part, as I don't think myself confined to any rules for Composition laid down by any that went before me, neither should I think (were I to pretend to lay down rules) that any man who comes after me were any ways obligated to adhere to them any further than they should think proper; so in fact I think it is best for every composer to be his own learner.

Much of Billings's work was directed at creating a new kind of hymn for the New England church; but his wrathful New England God, through a great outpouring of musical energy, was always enlisted on the side of independence and the revolutionary struggle. Here is one of Billings's first works, a setting of a passage from the "New England Hymn" by Rev. Dr. Byles. Appearing in 1770, it is an apt expression of the gathering American spirit.

America ¹⁰

Words: Rev. Dr. Byles **Music: William Billings**

See how the flocks of Jesus rise,
See how the Face of Paradise
Blooms through the Thickets of the Wild.
Here Liberty erects her Throne;
Here Plenty pours her Treasures down;
Peace smiles, as heav'nly Cherubs mild.

Lord, guard Thy Favors; Lord extend
Where farther Western suns descend;
Nor Southern Seas the Blessings bound;
Till Freedom lifts her cheerful Head,
Till pure Religion onward spread,
And beaming, wrap the Globe around.

No one event can cause a revolution, but a particular action can be the trigger that explodes a series of events into being. Such an action was the famous Boston Tea Party of December 16, 1773, which dumped $90,000 worth of tea to the bottom of Boston Harbor. The colonists' action was in response to a tax of threepence a pound levied on all tea imported to the Colonies, *despite the fact that the same tea was imported in England duty-free.* The colonists, already smarting from sundry confrontations with the crown on revenue and tax questions, saw the tea tax as a breach in their carefully constructed defenses against the depradations of the mother country. It is difficult to quarrel with their judgment, for the gain to the crown from the tea tax could, at best, have been only minimal. At first, Bostonians boycotted the hated tea, not because the tax made it particularly expensive, but for the reasons stated above. In fact, there was a brisk business in "black market" tea at the same time, even though colonists had to pay more for the smuggled tea. And while the tea-dumpers were clearly motivated by considerations of principle, there is good reason to believe that the concerns of at least some of the thinly disguised "Mohawks" who dumped 342 chests of tea into Boston Harbor went beyond revolutionary zeal to embrace more material financial considerations.

But the consequences of the raid were momentous, for with this bold act, the radicals won control of the independence forces in Boston. The British, in turn, responded by passing the "Intolerable Acts," including a measure to close the port of Boston until the destroyed tea was paid for. These acts also included provisions for trying capital crimes in England rather than the Colonies, and another measure virtually nullifying Massachusetts' charter. As a result, the colonists convoked the First Continental Congress to consider measures of support to Boston and concerted resistance to England.

The Destruction Of The Tea [11]

Words: Anonymous
Tune: "Hozier's Ghost"

1. As near beau-teous Bos-ton ly-ing, On the gen-tly__swell-ing flood,
With-out jack or__pen-nant fly-ing, Three ill-fat-ed__tea-ships rode, Just as__glo-rious Sol was set-ting, On the wharf, a num'-rous crew, Sons of free-dom,__fear for-get-ting, Sud-den-ly ap-peared in view.

Armed with hammers, axe and chisels,
Weapons new for warlike deed,
Towards the herbage-freighted vessels,
They approached with dreadful speed.

O'er their heads aloft in mid-sky,
Three bright angel forms were seen;
This was Hampden, that was Sidney,
With fair Liberty between.

"Soon," they cried, "your foes you'll banish,
Soon the triumph shall be won;
Scarce shall setting Phoebus vanish,
Ere the deathless deed be done."

Quick as thought the ships were boarded,
Hatches burst and chests displayed;
Axes, hammers, help afforded;
What a glorious crash they made.

Squash into the deep descended,
Cursed weed of China's coast;
Thus at once our fears were ended;
British rights shall ne'er be lost.

Captains! Once more hoist your streamers,
Spread your sails and plough the wave;
Tell your masters they were dreamers,
When they thought to cheat the brave.

In later years, the saga of the Boston Tea Party lent itself to songs of the music hall stage. The two songs that follow both postdate the Tea Party by at least half a century, but were much better known than the one above—lending some credence to the theory that a people's best revolutionary songs are frequently written after the battle is won.

Boston Tea Tax Song [12]

Words: Anonymous (ca. 1829)
Music: T. Comer

I__ snum I am a Yan-kee lad, And I guess I'll sing a dit-ty;__ And__
if you do not rel-ish it, The more 'twill be the pi-ty; That__
is, I think I should have been A pla-guey sight more fin-ished man If__
I'd been born in Bos-ton town, But I warn't 'cause I'm a coun-try-man, Tol-le-
lol-de-rid-dle, Tol-le-lol-de-ray, But I warn't 'cause I'm a coun-try-man.

And t'other day the Yankee folks
Were mad about the taxes,
And so we went like Injuns dressed
To split tea chests with axes.
It was the year of Seventy-three,
And we felt really gritty,
The Mayor he would have led the gang,
But Boston warn't a city!

You see we Yankees didn't care
A pin for wealth or booty,
And so in State Street we agreed
We'd never pay the duty;
That is, in State Street, 'twould have been,
But 'twas King Street they called it then,
And tax on tea, it was so bad,
The women wouldn't scald it then.

To Charleston Bridge we all went down
To see the thing corrected;
That is, we would have gone there,
But the bridge it warn't erected.
The tea, perhaps, was very good,
Bohea, Souchong or Hyson,
But drinking tea, it warn't the rage,
The duty made it poison.

And then aboard the ships we went
Our vengeance to administer,
And we didn't care one tarnal bit
For any king or minister.
We made a plaguey mess of tea
In one of the biggest dishes;
I mean we steeped it in the sea
And treated all the fishes.

And then, you see, we were all found out,
A thing we hadn't dreaded.
The leaders were to London sent
And instantly beheaded.
That is, I mean, they would have been,
If ever they'd been taken,
But the leaders they were never cotched,
And so they saved their bacon.

Now heaven bless the president
And all this goodly nation,
And doubly bless our Boston mayor
And all the corporation;
And may all those who are our foes,
Or at our praise have faltered,
Soon have a change—that is, I mean,
May all of them get haltered.

Revolutionary Tea [13]

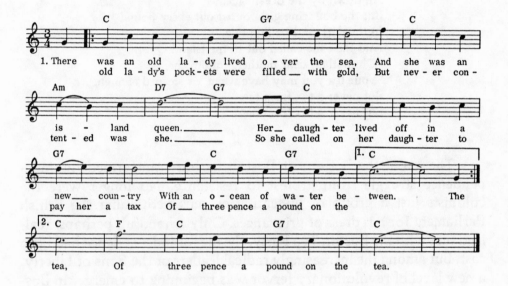

1. There was an old la-dy lived o-ver the sea, And she was an
   old la-dy's pock-ets were filled with gold, But nev-er con-

   is-land queen. Her daugh-ter lived off in a
   tent-ed was she. So she called on her daugh-ter to

   new coun-try With an o-cean of wa-ter be-tween. The
   pay her a tax Of three pence a pound on the

   tea, Of three pence a pound on the tea.

"Now mother, dear mother," the daughter replied,
"I shan't do the thing that you ax;
I'm willing to pay a fair price for the tea,
But never the three-penny tax."
"You shall," quoth the mother, and reddened with rage,
"For you're my own daughter, you see.
And sure 'tis quite proper the daughter should pay
Her mother a tax on the tea,
Her mother a tax on the tea."

And so the old lady her servant called up,
And packed off a budget of tea,
And eager for three pence a pound, she put in
Enough for a large family.
She ordered her servant to bring home the tax
Declaring her child should obey,
Or old as she was, and a woman most grown,
She'd half whip her life away,
She'd half whip her life away.

The tea was conveyed to the daughter's door,
All down by the ocean side,
But the bouncing girl poured out every pound
In the dark and boiling tide.
And then she called out to the Island Queen,
"Oh mother, dear mother," quoth she,
"Your tea you may have when 'tis steeped enough,
But never a tax from me,
But never a tax from me."

The tea at the bottom of Boston harbor transformed the independence struggle from protest to resistance. No longer were the colonists just a group of dissenting citizens petitioning the British Parliament for a redress of grievances. Only a handful, perhaps, realized that with the Boston Tea Party, the die for independence had been cast. But among the increasingly radical leaders of the Sons of Liberty, a new level of revolutionary fervor was beginning to emerge. In Boston, Dr. Joseph Warren,[14] a central figure in the period of revolutionary agitation, captured the new spirit with an anthem that was more militantly radical than any earlier expression.

In writing his anthem, Dr. Warren was perhaps emboldened by the fact that many prominent people in England were sympathetic to the American cause. Among them was Edward Gibbon, author of *The Decline and Fall of the Roman Empire* and a member of Parliament at the time. Warren might very well have been thinking of Gibbon and his work when he included the references to antiquity in the first verse of his song.

The song appeared in colonial newspapers in 1774. Warren, himself, was later killed at the Battle of Bunker Hill at the age of thirty-four.

Free America [15]

Words: Joseph Warren
Tune: "The British Grenadiers"

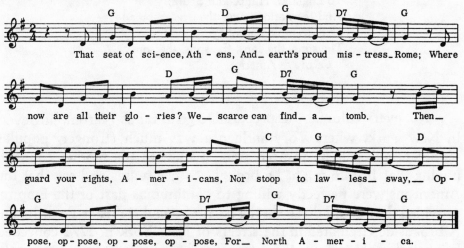

That seat of sci-ence, Ath - ens, And earth's proud mis - tress Rome; Where now are all their glo - ries? We scarce can find a tomb. Then guard your rights, A - mer - i - cans, Nor stoop to law - less sway, Op - pose, op - pose, op - pose, op - pose, For North A - mer - i - ca.

We led fair Freedom hither,
And lo, the desert smiled!
A paradise of pleasure
Was opened in the wild!
Your harvest, bold Americans,
No power shall snatch away!
Huzza, huzza, huzza, huzza,
    For free America.

Torn from a world of tyrants,
Beneath this western sky,
We formed a new dominion,
A land of liberty.
The world shall own we're masters here,
Then hasten on the day:
Oppose, oppose, oppose, oppose,
    For free America.

Lift up your hands, ye heroes,
And swear with proud disdain,
The wretch that would ensnare you,
Shall lay his snares in vain:
Should Europe empty all her force,
We'll meet her in array,
And fight and shout, and shout and fight
    For North America.

Some future day shall crown us
The masters of the main,
Our fleets shall speak in thunder
To England, France and Spain;
And the nations over the ocean spread
Shall tremble and obey
The sons, the sons, the sons, the sons
    Of brave America.

Not every colonial was prepared to go as far as Warren, however. In New York, where Tory influence was much stronger, popular sentiment still sought an accommodation with the mother country, hoping that Britain might be brought to her senses and see that the Americans were perfectly willing to continue as part of the Empire, provided they could do so on the basis of equal rights as Englishmen. A broadside circulated in the streets of New York in 1774 conceded Britannia's right to "rule the waves," and pledged cooperation if only the mother country would understand that her "free-born sons will ne'er be slaves."

The American Rule Britannia [16]

Words: Anonymous
Tune: "Rule Britannia"

1. When Brit-ons first, by Heav'n's com-mand, A-rose from out the az-ure main, A-rose from out the az-ure main,

This was the char-ter, the char-ter of the land, And guard-ian an — gels sang this strain: Rule, Bri-tan-nia, Bri-tan-nia rule the waves, Brit — ons nev-er, nev-er, nev-er nev — er shall be slaves. shall be slaves.

To spread bright freedom's gentle sway,
Your isle too narrow for its bound,
We traced wild ocean's trackless way,
And here a safe asylum found.
   Rule Britannia, Britannia rule the waves,
   But know thy sons will ne'er be slaves.

While we were simple, you grew great;
Now swelled with luxury and pride,
You pierce our peaceful free retreat
And haste t'enslave with giant stride.
   Rule Britannia, Britannia rule the waves,
   But free-born sons will ne'er be slaves.

Thee haughty tyrants ne'er could tame;
All their attempts to pull thee down
Did but arouse thy grievous flame,
And work their woe and thy renown.
   Rule Britannia, Britannia rule the waves,
   But know thy sons will ne'er be slaves.

Let us, your sons, by freedom warmed,
Your own example keep in view—
'Gainst tyranny be ever armed,
Though we our tyrants find—in you.
　Rule Britannia, Britannia rule the waves,
　Thy free-born sons will ne'er be slaves.

With justice and with wisdom reign,
We then with thee will firmly join,
To make thee mistress of the main,
And every shore it circles, thine.
　Rule Britannia, Britannia rule the waves,
　Thy children never will be slaves.

When life glides slowly through thy veins,
We'll then our filial fondness prove,
Bound only by the welcome chains
Of duty, gratitude and love.
　Rule Britannia, Britannia rule the waves,
　Depend on children—not on slaves.

Our youth shall prop thy tottering age;
Our vigor nerve thy feeble arm.
In vain thy foes shall spend their rage—
We'll shield thee safe from every harm.
　Rule Britannia, Britannia rule the waves,
　Confide in children—not in slaves.

For thee we'll toil with cheerful heart;
We'll labor—*but we will be free,*
Our growth and strength to thee impart,
And all our treasure bring to thee.
　Rule Britannia, Britannia rule the waves,
　Thou nor thy sons shall e'er be slaves.

While the dumping of the tea in Boston accelerated the development of revolutionary consciousness, the British crown reacted with dispatch and severity. The Tory-controlled Parliament flew into an uproar when the news from Boston reached London. "Boston ought to be knocked about their ears and destroyed," stormed one member, who proposed that the army "burn and set fire to all their woods." A series of actions by the British, designed to punish the rebellious colonials and to restore law and order, only aggravated the situation.

First, the port of Boston was closed. No commerce could go in or out by sea, thus immediately throttling the town's chief business activity. British warships dropped anchor in Boston harbor to enforce the ban. The port was to remain closed until the tea had been paid for and the royal authority was convinced that the citizenry would obey future orders of the crown. These measures were supplemented by a number of other acts—immediately dubbed the "Intolerable Acts" by the Americans—designed to break the growing spirit of independence in the Massachusetts Bay Colony.

What the British did not expect, however, was that the other American colonies would come to the aid of the Massachusetts rebels. But food and provisions poured into Boston from as far as Virginia and the Carolinas. When Boston laborers refused to construct new barracks for the British army, General Gage went to New York to recruit workers; these, in turn, refused to take the employment as an act of solidarity. Anticipating the developing confrontation, minutemen organizations were formed, with the citizenry of all the Colonies arming themselves and preparing for conflict. The Virginia House of Burgesses was dissolved by the governor after acts of support to blockaded Boston, and responded, in turn, by calling the First Continental Congress, which met in Philadelphia, September 5, 1774.

Meanwhile, General Thomas Gage, commander of the British troops in North America and military governor of Massachusetts, had sent to England for reinforcements. These were not long in coming. Britain had no intention of losing her prized North American possessions. A 1775 song of love and separation in which the young man was sent to fight the rebels in North America became popular both in England and America.

The Banks Of The Dee [17]

Words: John Tait [18]
Tune: Adapted from "Langolee"

> 'Twas summer and softly the breezes were blowing,
> And sweetly the nightingale sang from the tree.
> At the foot of a hill, where the river was flowing,
> I sat myself down on the banks of the Dee.
> Flow on, lovely Dee, flow on thou sweet river,
> Thy banks, purest stream, shall be dear to me ever,
> For there I first gained the affection and favor
> Of Jamie, the glory and pride of the Dee.

But now he's gone from me and left me thus mourning,
To quell the proud rebels, for valiant is he;
But ah! there's no hope of his speedy returning,
To wander again on the banks of the Dee:
He's gone, hapless youth, o'er the rude roaring billows,
The kindest, the sweetest, of all his brave fellows;
And left me to stray 'mongst these once loved willows,
The loneliest lass on the banks of the Dee.

But time and my prayers may perhaps yet restore him,
Blest peace may restore my dear lover to me,
And when he returns with such care I'll watch o'er him,
He never shall leave the sweet banks of the Dee.
The Dee then will flow, all its beauty displaying,
The lambs on its banks will again be seen playing,
Whilst I, with my Jamie, am carelessly straying,
And tasting again all the sweets of the Dee.

But the colonists could not be expected to have an abundance of sympathy for poor Jamie sent to "quell the proud rebels." A Connecticut rhymester, Oliver Arnold, a relative of the famous traitor, responded with a parody on the popular air:

The Banks Of The Dee (parody) [19]

Words: Oliver Arnold
Tune: "The Banks of the Dee"

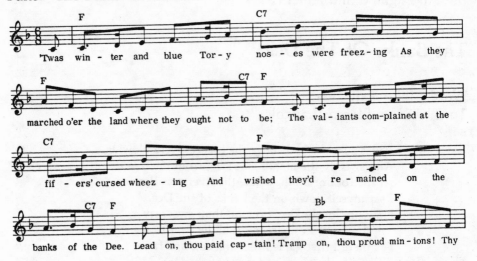

'Twas win-ter and blue Tor-y nos-es were freez-ing As they marched o'er the land where they ought not to be; The val-iants com-plained at the fif-ers' cursed wheez-ing And wished they'd re-mained on the banks of the Dee. Lead on, thou paid cap-tain! Tramp on, thou proud min-ions! Thy

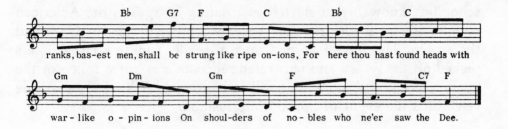

ranks, bas-est men, shall be strung like ripe on-ions, For here thou hast found heads with war - like o - pin - ions On shoul-ders of no - bles who ne'er saw the Dee.

Prepare for war's conflict; or make preparation
For peace with the rebels, for they're brave and glee;
Keep mindful of dying, and leave the foul nation
That sends out its armies to brag and to flee.
Make haste, now, and leave us thou miscreant tories!
To Scotland repair! there court the sad houris,
And listen once more to their plaints and their stories
Concerning the "glory and pride of the Dee."

Be quiet and sober, secure and contented,
Upon your own land, be valiant and free;
Bless God that the war is so nicely prevented,
And till the green fields on the banks of the Dee.
The Dee then will flow, all its beauty displaying,
The lads on its banks will again be seen playing,
And England thus honestly taxes defraying,
With natural drafts from the banks of the Dee.

And so the stage was set for direct armed confrontation between an increasingly angry and rebellious America and a reinforced British garrison army. While the colonists stored up arms and munitions in the New England countryside and revolutionary agitation reached new heights of passion, General Gage decided to strike a preemptive blow against the rebels.

Gage's immediate target was a store of military supplies the colonists had accumulated at the town of Concord in Massachusetts; and so on the night of April 18, 1775, the British general ordered his troops out of their stronghold in Boston for a midnight march on that historic town. The events of the next two days mark the beginning of the military aspect of the American struggle for independence. Paul Revere's dash through the Massachusetts countryside, the embattled farmers at Lexington, the Concord Bridge—all these have become a part of those legends on which a people's history is built. For, as every schoolboy knows, what started as a daring foray into the American countryside by British regulars became a bitter defeat for Gage and the crown. The retreat from Concord while Yankee sharpshooters picked off the weary and frustrated redcoats was but a token of the years to come and the battles still to be fought. A Yankee broadside celebrated the event in appropriate fashion.

The Irishman's Epistle [20]

Tune: "The Irish Washerwoman"

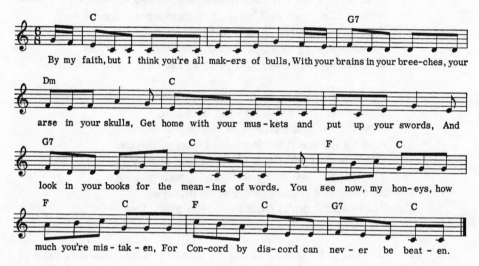

By my faith, but I think you're all mak-ers of bulls, With your brains in your bree-ches, your arse in your skulls, Get home with your mus-kets and put up your swords, And look in your books for the mean-ing of words. You see now, my hon-eys, how much you're mis-tak-en, For Con-cord by dis-cord can nev-er be beat-en.

How brave ye went out with your muskets all bright,
And thought to befrighten the folks with the sight;
But when you got there how they powdered your pums,
And all the way home how they peppered your bums;
And is it not, honeys, a comical crack,
To be proud in the face and be shot in the back.

With all of your talkin' and all of your wordin',
And all of your shoutin' and marchin' and swordin', [21]
How come ye to think now they didn't know how
To be after their firelocks as smartly as you?
You see now, my honeys, 'tis nothing at all,
But to pull at the trigger and pop goes the ball.

And what have you got now with all your designing,
But a town without victuals to sit down and dine in;
And to look on the ground like a parcel of noodles,
And sing, how the Yankees have beaten the Doodles.
I'm sure if you're wise you'll make peace for a dinner,
For fighting and fasting will soon make you thinner.

The battles at Lexington and Concord reversed the military situation in Massachusetts. When Gage's troops went marching out into the New England countryside the night of April 18, they had successfully blockaded the port of Boston for almost a year. When they returned, they entered a city that was immediately placed under a siege by the newly formed rebel army. Other battles would follow—some of them, like Bunker Hill, nominal British victories; but the situation had been inexorably changed. After Concord, the British were invaders in a hostile land.

Symptomatic of this change was the arrival in Boston harbor on May 25 of the H.M.S. *Cerberus*. The British frigate, named for the dog that, in Greek mythology, guarded the gates of Hell, was launched from Britain with a popular verse reflecting the cynicism of some, at least, to imperial policy:

Behold the Cerberus the Atlantic plough,
Her precious cargo: Burgoyne, Clinton, Howe.
Bow, wow, wow!

The three generals, all of them, incidentally, members of Parliament, represented George III's determination to hold his American possessions and to keep them subject to British rule. Ironically, Sir William Howe, who became the commander of British troops in North America, was not without sympathy for the colonists' cause. In politics he was a Whig and he had condemned the government's North American policies in the Parliament. At one point he had even written a letter to a certain Mr. Kirk saying that he would never accept a position of command against the colonists. But in February of 1775, after receiving his orders, he wrote to the same Kirk: "My going thither was not of my seeking. I was ordered, and could not refuse, without incurring the odious name of backwardness to serve my country in distress."

The arrival of the three generals unleashed a flood of denuncia-

65

tion from the Americans and undoubtedly contributed to the consolidation of the Revolutionary cause. A number of satiric broadside songs welcomed this military "junto."

A Junto Song [22]

Words: Anonymous
Tune: "A-begging We Will Go"

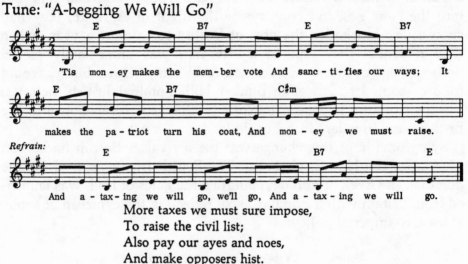

'Tis mon-ey makes the mem-ber vote And sanc-ti-fies our ways; It makes the pa-triot turn his coat, And mon-ey we must raise.

Refrain:

And a-tax-ing we will go, we'll go, And a-tax-ing we will go.

More taxes we must sure impose,
To raise the civil list;
Also pay our ayes and noes,
And make opposers hist.

One single thing untaxed at home,
Old England could not show,
For money we abroad did roam,
And thought to tax the *new*.

The power supreme of Parliament,
Our purpose did assist,
And taxing laws abroad were sent,
Which rebels do resist.

Shall we not make the rascals bend
To Britain's supreme power?
The sword shall we not to them send,
And leaden balls a-shower?

Boston we shall in ashes lay,
It is a nest of knaves:
We'll make them soon for mercy pray,
Or send them to their graves.

But second thoughts are ever best,
And lest our force should fail,
What fraud can do, we'll make a test,
And see what bribes avail.

Each colony, we will propose,
Shall raise an ample sum;
Which well applied, under the rose,
May bribe them—as at home.

We'll force and fraud in one unite,
To bring them to our hands;
Then lay a tax on the sun's light,
And king's tax on their lands.

Another "junto" song, while acknowledging that some in England—the Earl of Chatham (William Pitt), Chief Justice Lord Camden and various members of Parliament—had opposed the royal policy towards North America, stated in the boldest terms that "there's no cure but a capital chop."

Fish And Tea[23]

Words: Anonymous
Tune: "Derry Down"

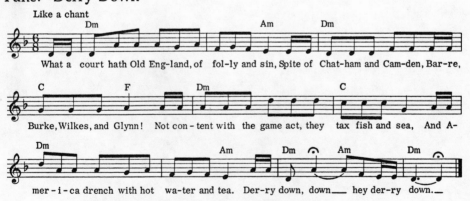

What a court hath Old Eng-land, of fol-ly and sin, Spite of Chat-ham and Cam-den, Bar-re, Burke, Wilkes, and Glynn! Not con-tent with the game act, they tax fish and sea, And A-mer-i-ca drench with hot wa-ter and tea. Der-ry down, down__ hey der-ry down.__

But if the wise council of England doth think
They may be enslaved by the power of drink,
They're right to enforce it; but then do you see?
The Colonies, too, may refuse and be free.

There's no knowing where this oppression will stop;
Some say there's no cure but a capital chop;
And that I believe's each American's wish,
Since you've drenched them with tea and deprived 'em of fish. [24]

The birds of the air and the fish of the sea,
By the gods for poor Dan Adam's use were made free,
Till a man with more power than old Moses would wish,
Said, "Ye wretches, ye shan't touch a fowl or a fish!"

Three generals these mandates have borne 'cross the sea,
To deprive 'em of fish and make 'em drink tea;
In turn, sure, these freemen will boldly agree,
To give 'em a dance upon Liberty Tree.

Then *freedom's* the word, both at home and abroad,
And damn every scabbard that hides a good sword!
Our forefathers gave us this freedom in hand,
And we'll die in defense of the rights of the land.
    Derry down, down, hey derry down.

Yankee Doodles

Songs of Rebels and Patriots,
Foot Soldiers and Revolutionary Heroes

The War for American Independence is not particularly considered a "singing war." Certainly not like the Civil War which corresponded to a line of cultural demarcation from which a distinctively American music emerged.

The Civil War songs which had a lasting impact on our consciousness are varied and numerous: anthems such as "Battle Hymn of the Republic," "Battle Cry of Freedom" and "Bonnie Blue Flag"; marching songs like "John Brown's Body," "When Johnny Comes Marching Home," "Marching Through Georgia" and "Tramp, Tramp, Tramp"; sentimental songs such as "Weeping Sad and Lonely," "Just Before the Battle, Mother," "Tenting Tonight," "The Vacant Chair" and scores of others.

By contrast, the Revolution's musical legacy is on the thin side. Except for "Yankee Doodle" and possibly William Billings's "Chester," few songs of that era have survived the passage of time. The reasons for this are fairly obvious. At the time of the Revolution, no real musical base had been established in the Colonies. The music the colonists knew was largely imported from England. The small, predominantly rural-based population had not yet developed the technology for widespread circulation of music nor were there any more than a handful who could make a living as professional musicians. Add to this the severe strictures against "entertainments" which were a part of the religious background of many and the particular nature of the sometimes positional, sometimes guerrilla war fought by the rebels, and the number of songs actually produced during the period becomes fairly impressive.

The need of any revolution to demystify the symbols of once-sacred authority gives rise to a cultural atmosphere of nonconformity and iconoclasm which from time to time seems to verge on perversity. Surely some devil-may-care spirit of defiant levelism spawned by the resistance to King and Parliament helps to account for the fact that the Revolution's most popular song—indeed, virtually its only true folk song—was "Yankee Doodle."

The origins of "Yankee Doodle" have long since been obscured by history. A variety of wildly improbable theories, some of them purporting to date the tune back to Cromwell's time, and one, at least, which suggests that this might have been the tune Nero fiddled while Rome burned, have been largely discredited.

It was widely known as an instrumental melody by the middle of the eighteenth century, popular as a tune for jigs and contra dances, and may well have been "invented" by some early American fiddler who either made it up whole or, as seems more likely, "composed" it in the framework of the common musical idiom of the time.

Theories concerning the origin of the term "Yankee Doodle" are also diverse and difficult to substantiate. Some have suggested that the word "Yankee" derived from the Indian pronunciation of the word "English," or from the French word for the English, *Anglais.* "Doodle," on the other hand, was long in use as a derisive term, meaning dolt or simpleton.

There is much to commend this theory since it corresponds so well to the usual attitudes of people from the mother country towards colonial settlers. The first lyrics associated with the song, and the grandfather of the now-standardized version known as "The Yankee's

Return from Camp," likewise reflect this attitude of good-natured contempt for the Yankee rubes and rustics encountered by the "cultured" English military officers who came to North America during the French and Indian War.

In fact, it is precisely from that period that the first "Yankee Doodle" came. Theory has it that it was the work of a British army surgeon, Dr. Richard Shuckburg, who is said to have written the lyrics while serving with the army of General Amherst in upper New York. Oscar Sonneck, chief of the Music Division of the Library of Congress for many years, extensively researched the song's origins and concluded that the story about Shuckburg having written it in 1755 could not be proved. Subsequently, John Tasker Howard, probably our most distinguished music historian, suggested that there might be some merit to the claim for Shuckburg but that the date might be 1758.

Whether the British doctor wrote this first version or merely adapted the verses from some in popular currency, it seems certain that he had something to do with the first "Yankee Doodle." It's an indelicate composition, and many music historians found the last two verses too strong for their taste and refused to commit them to print. The Yankee—Brother Ephraim—is clearly the butt of this song, and the general tone of the verses is certainly consistent with the attitude of tolerant scorn which many a British officer had towards his American cousins.

Yankee Doodle [1]

Words: Dr. Richard Schuckburg
Tune: "Yankee Doodle"

> Brother Ephraim sold his cow
> And bought him a commission,
> And then he went to Canada
> To fight for the nation;
> But when Ephraim, he came home,
> He proved an arrant coward,
> He wouldn't fight the Frenchmen there
> For fear of being devoured.

Sheep's head and vinegar,
Buttermilk and tansy,
Boston is a Yankee town,
Sing "Hey, doodle dandy!"
First we'll take a pinch of snuff,
And then a drink of water,
And then we'll say, "How do you do?"
And that's a Yankee supper.

Aminadab is just come home,
His eyes all greased with bacon,
And all the news that he could tell
Is Cape Breton is taken.
Stand up Jonathan,
Figure in by neighbor,
Father stand a little off
And make the room some wider.

Christmas is a-coming, boys,
We'll go to Mother Chase's,
And there we'll get a sugar dram
Sweetened with melasses:
Heigh ho for our Cape Cod,
Heigh ho Nantasket,
Do not let the Boston wags
Feel your oyster basket.

Punkin pie is very good
And so is apple lantern,
Had you been whipp'd as oft as I
You'd not have been so wanton.
Uncle is a Yankee man,
In faith, he pays us all off,
And he has got a fiddle
As big as daddy's hog's trough.

Seth's mother went to Lynn
To buy a pair of breeches,
The first time father put them on
He tore out all the stitches;
Dolly Bushel let a fart,
Jenny Jones she found it,
Ambrose carried it to mill
Where Doctor Warren ground it.

> Our Jemina's lost her mare
> And can't tell where to find her,
> But she'll come trotting by and by
> And bring her tail behind her.
> Two and two may go to bed,
> Two and two together,
> And if there is not room enough,
> Lie one a top o' t'other.

The first time this "Yankee Doodle" appeared in print was 1775 in London, where its printer, Thomas Skillern, subtitled it "The Lexington March." The reason for the subtitle was that the British army band fifed it while the troops were on their way to Lexington, giving rise to the legend that a New England boy standing by the roadside in Roxbury shouted out to General Percy, leading a relief column to the battle scene: "You go out to Yankee Doodle, but you will dance by and by to Chevy Chase!" The exclamation strikes one as a little pat, however, since it presupposes in addition to a familiarity with the circumstances of the old ballad of "Chevy Chase" in which a certain Earl Henry Percy lost a famous battle in 1388, that the lad knew the British general's name.

Skillern's broadside suggests that "the words... be sung thro' the Nose, & in the West Country drawl & dialect." Some historians have seen the publication of the broadside at that time and with the subtitle as an expression of solidarity between some in Britain and the rebels. But this presupposes that most Englishmen looked at the Lexington march the same way history has, that is, as a defeat for the British. There is little evidence that Londoners maintained such a view at that time, and commercial exploitation of a timely event seems the much more likely explanation than any ideological affinity with the rebel cause.

But the song was immensely popular throughout the Colonies long before 1775, and there is good reason to believe that it was already somewhat known by word of mouth and also by melody in England. Andrew Barton's ballad opera, *The Disappointment*, scheduled to be performed in Philadelphia April 20, 1767, and precipitously cancelled because "it contains personal reflections," makes mention of the tune in the stage directions. In 1770, a political satire, *The Procession*, likewise refers to "Yankee Doodle" and includes some stanzas suggesting both the older comic song and the later rebel song.

An undated broadside, apparently of the early seventies, provides the model for what later became the standard version of the song. What is important about this intermediary song is that its first two verses are clearly derived from the original "Yankee Doodle" while its subsequent stanzas were adapted to and incorporated in the later version. The song has eighteen verses, but a few will suffice to make the point:

Yankee Song [2]

Tune: "Yankee Doodle"

There is a man in our town,
I'll tell you his condition,
He sold his oxen and his cows
To buy him a commission.

Chorus:
Corn-stalks twist your hair off,
Cart-wheel frolic round you,
Old fiery dragon carry you off,
And mortar pessel pound you.

When a commission he had got,
He proved to be a coward,
He durst not go to Canada
For fear of being devoured.

But father and I went down to camp
Along with Captain Goodwin,
And there we saw the men and boys
As thick as hasty pudding.

And there they had a little keg,
The heads were made of leather,
They rap't upon't with little clubs
To call the folks together.

There I saw a swamping gun
As big's a log of maple,
Put upon two little wheels
A load for father's cattle.

I saw a man a-talking there
You might heard to the barn, sir,
Hallooing and scolding too—
The deal of one would answer.

There he kept a-riding round
Upon a spanking stallion,
And all the people standing round,
A thousand or a million.

Brother Si is gone to town
With a load of shingles,
And if he can't have lasses for't,
He vows he'll breed a wrangle.

For brother Jo is come to town,
He's gone to knock them all off,
He plays upon a swamping fiddle
As big as father's hog trough.

Now husking time is over,
They have a deuced frolic,
There'll be some as drunk as sots,
The rest will have the colic.

In addition to its obvious connections with both the early and later versions, the song above is interesting, too, because it introduces the common image of Yankee Doodle going to town, although here it is brothers Si and Jonathan.

One stanza apparently popular with the Tories and supposedly sung by the British troops on the way to Lexington went:

Yankee Doodle's come to town
For to buy a firelock,
We will tar and feather him,
And so we will John Hancock.

Later versions of the song abounded in the same theme, although none of these can be firmly dated to the Revolutionary period. The most widely known stanza, in fact, does not appear anywhere in print until 1852:

Yankee Doodle came to town
Riding on a pony,
He stuck a feather in his hat
And called it macaroni.

But it was a Harvard sophomore, Edward Bangs, who put together the version of "Yankee Doodle" which has become best known to history. Bangs was a Minuteman who is said to have participated in the events of April 19, 1775, but there are no hard facts as to when he actually compiled the song. The internal evidence would indicate that the song could not have been written before July 3, 1775, since it was on that day that Washington took command of the American army in Boston. The stanza calling Washington "so tarnal proud" is an interesting reflection of a class attitude which was to surface from time to time in other songs of the period.

The Yankee's Return From Camp [3]

Words: Edward Bangs
Tune: "Yankee Doodle"

Fath'r and I went down to camp, A - long with Cap - tain Good - ing; And there we saw the men and boys As thick as hast - y pud - ding.

Chorus:
Yan - kee Doo - dle, keep it up, Yan - kee Doo - dle dan - dy;
Mind the mu - sic and the step And with the girls be han - dy.

And there we see a thousand men
As rich as Squire David,
And what they wasted every day,
I wish it could be savéd.

The 'lasses they eat every day
Would keep a house a winter;
They have as much that I'll be bound
They eat it when they're a mind to.

And there we see a swamping gun,
Large as a log of maple,
Upon a deuced little cart,
A load for father's cattle.

And every time they shoot it off,
It takes a horn of powder,
It makes a noise like father's gun,
Only a nation louder.

I went as nigh to one myself,
As 'Siah's underpinning;
And father went as nigh afain,
I thought the deuce was in him.

Cousin Simon grew so bold,
I thought he would have cocked it;
It scared me so, I shrieked it off,
And hung by father's pocket.

And Captain Davis had a gun,
He kind of clapped his hand on't,
And stuck a crooked stabbing iron
Upon the little end on't.

And there I see a pumpkin-shell
As big as mother's baisin,
And every time they touched it off
They scampered like the nation.

I see a little barrel, too,
The heads were made of leather,
They knocked upon with little clubs,
And called the folks together.

And there was Captain Washington,
And gentle folks about him;
They say he's grown so tarnal proud
He will not ride without them.

He got him on his meeting-clothes,
Upon a slapping stallion,
He set the world along in rows,
In hundreds and in millions.

The flaming ribbons in his hat,
They looked so taring fine, ah,
I wanted pockily to get
To give to my Jemimah.

I see another snarl of men,
A-digging graves they told me,
So tarnal long, so tarnal deep,
They 'tended they should hold me.

It scared me so I hooked it off,
Nor stopped as I remember,
Nor turned about till I got home,
Locked up in mother's chamber.

There is no way to tabulate all the verses and variations which the ingenious rebels created during the years of the Revolution. And while the tune was appropriated by the colonists, many a Tory seized on the catchy melody to pen a verse expressing loyalty to King George or derision for the Continental Congress.

One New York Loyalist joined the musical fray just as soon as the news of Washington's appointment to command of the continental armies became known. The anonymous bard seems to see Washington as somewhat resembling a Don Quixote figure, a third-rate aristocrat whose wig is sunburnt and more concerned with "counting specie" than leading his armies. In a footnote to the song, the author suggests that Washington's horse, Lily, was really a donkey and that its name derived from "the whiteness of its hide, which was pretty well-exposed to the weather . . . and by mange." Lawyer Close may be a veiled reference to Washington's aide, Major General Charles Lee, while the "patriot dinner" of the last line refers, again in the words of the song's author, to "corn pudding and Yankee rum, a great promoter of rebellion and riot."

Adam's Fall (or The Trip To Cambridge) [4]

Author: Anonymous
Tune: "Yankee Doodle"

When Congress sent great Washington,
All clothed in power and breeches,
To meet old Britain's warlike sons
And make some rebel speeches;

'Twas then he took his gloomy way
Astride his dapple donkeys,
And travelled well, both night and day,
Until he reached the Yankees.

Away from camp, 'bout three miles off,
From Lily he dismounted,
His sergeant brushed his sun-burnt wig,
While he the specie counted.

All prinked up in full bag-wig,
The shaking notwithstanding,
In leathers tight, oh! glorious sight!
He reached the Yankee landing.

The women ran, the darkeys too,
And all the bells they tolléd;
For Britain's sons, by Doodle doo,
We're sure to be—consoléd.

Old mother Hancock with a pan
All crowded full of butter,
Unto the lovely Georgius ran,
And added to the splutter.

Says she, "Our brindle has just calved,
And John is wondrous happy,
He sent this present to you, dear,
As you're the 'country's papa.'"

"You'll butter bread and bread butter,
But do not butt your speeches,
You'll butter bread and bread butter,
But do not grease your breeches."

Full many a child went into camp,
All dressed in homespun kersey, [5]
To see the greatest rebel scamp
That ever crossed o'er Jersey.

The rebel clowns, oh! what a sight!
Too awkward was their figure;
'Twas yonder stood a pious wight,
And here and there a nigger.

Upon a stump he placed himself,
Great Washington did he,
And through the nose of Lawyer Close,
Proclaimed great Liberty.

The patriot brave, the patriot fair,
From fever had grown thinner,
So off they marched with patriot zeal,
And took a patriot dinner.

Such Tory verses did not discourage the rebels from using their tune, however. For every Loyalist stanza there were a hundred improvised by Yankee bards. One popular verse which served the rebels well summed it all up:

Yankee Doodle is the tune,
That we all delight in;
It suits for feasts, it suits for fun,
And just as well for fightin'.

But "Yankee Doodle" wasn't the only tune the rebels captured from the crown. Most of their tunes, of course, were English, Scottish or Irish. Even the British anthem, "God Save the King," provided the Americans with a melody for their verses. Two such make reference to General Richard Montgomery, who was an early hero of the Revolutionary cause. Son of an Irish MP, Montgomery developed liberal political views and emigrated to America in 1772, after having seen service in Canada during the French and Indian War. He quickly became active in colonial affairs and was a delegate to the first provincial congress in New York. In 1775 he accepted appointment as a brigadier general in the Continental Army and led an offensive into Canada which succeeded in capturing St. Johns and Montreal. Montgomery was killed during the unsuccessful attack on Quebec on December 31, 1775.

God Save America[6]

Tune: "God Save the King"

God save A - mer - i - ca, Free from des - pot - ic sway,
Till time shall end. Hushed be the din of arms, And to fierce
war's a - larms; Show in all its charms Heav - en born peace.

God save great Washington,
Fair freedom's warlike son,
Long to command.
May every enemy,
Far from his presence flee,
And may grim tyranny
Fall by his hand.

Thy name Montgomery,
Still in each heart shall be
Praised in each breast.
Though on the fatal plain
Thou most untimely slain,
Yet shall thy virtue's gain
Rescue from death.

Last in our song shall be,
Guardian of liberty,
Louis the King.
Terrible god of war,
Placed in victorious carr [7]
Of fame and of Navarre;
God save the King.

The last verse is a reference to the aid which came from France after the conclusion of the alliance between the French and the Colonists in 1778. The irony of the rebels singing "God save the King" as their last line, meaning the king of France and not England, is self-evident.

Another parody to "God Save the King" is attributed to "a Dutch lady at the Hague, for the sailors of the five American vessels at Amsterdam." The song appeared in the *Pennsylvania Packet* in 1779.

God Save The Thirteen States [8]

Tune: "God Save the King"

God save the Thirteen States!
Long rule th' United States!
God save our States!
Make us victorious,
Happy and glorious,
No tyrants over us;
God save our States!

To our famed Washington,
Brave Stark at Bennington,
Glory is due.
Peace to Montgomery's shade,
Who as he fought and bled,
Drew honors 'round his head,
Num'rous as true.

We'll fear no tyrant's nod,
Nor stern oppression's rod,
Till time's no more.
This Liberty, when driv'n
From Europe's states, is giv'n
A safe retreat and hav'n,
On our free shore.

Oh, Lord! Thy gifts in store,
We pray on Congress pour,
To guide our States.
May union bless our land,
While we with heart and hand,
Our mutual rights defend,
God save our States!

One Revolutionary song came close to becoming the anthem of the colonial cause. William Billings's "Chester" was extremely popular among the rebel troops, especially those from New England, who are reported to have sung it constantly throughout the war. An earlier version of the hymn had been composed by Billings about 1770. But with the outbreak of hostilities, the Boston singing master adapted his song to the temper of revolutionary ardor.

Chester[9]

Words and music: William Billings

Like a march (not too slow)

1. Let ty-rants shake their i - ron rod, And slav-'ry clank her gall - ing chains. We fear them not; we trust in God: New Eng-land's God for - ev - er reigns.

Howe and Burgoyne, and Clinton, too,
With Prescott [10] and Cornwallis joined,
Together plot our overthrow,
In one infernal league combined.

When God inspired us for the fight,
Their ranks were broke, their lines were forced;
Their ships were shattered in our sight,
Or swiftly driven from our coast.

The foe comes on with haughty stride,
Our troops advance with martial noise;
Their veterans flee before our youth,
And generals yield to beardless boys.

What grateful offering shall we bring?
What shall we render to the Lord?
Loud hallelujahs let us sing,
And praise his name on every chord.

One of the most explicitly revolutionary songs was the work of Dr. Jonathan Mitchell Sewall of New Hampshire, author of many poems and ballads dealing with the issues of the time. Sewall was of a distinguished New England family. He was the adopted son of Chief Justice Stephen Sewall of Massachusetts and, thereby, a grandnephew of Samuel Sewall, the widely respected man of letters, merchant and colonial magistrate. He also wrote "War and Washington."

On Independence [11]

Words: Jonathan Mitchell Sewall
Tune: "The Jam on Gerry's Rocks" [12]

In a cause that's so righteous, come let us agree,
And from hostile invaders, set America free;
The cause is so glorious, we need not to fear,
But from merciless tyrants we'll set ourselves clear.

Heaven's blessing attending us, no tyrant shall say,
That Americans e'er to such monsters gave way,
But fighting we'll die in America's cause,
Before we'll submit to tyrannical laws.

George the Third of Great Britain, no more shall he reign,
With unlimited sway o'er these free States again,
Lord North, nor old Bute, nor none of their clan,
Shall ever be honored by an American.

84

May heaven's blessings descend on our United States,
And grant that the union may never abate;
May love, peace, and harmony ever be found,
For to go hand in hand America round.

Upon our grand Congress may heaven bestow
Both wisdom and skill our good to pursue;
On Heaven alone, dependent we'll be,
But from all earthly tyrants we mean to be free.

Unto our brave generals may heaven give skill,
Our armies to guide and the sword for to wield,
May their hands taught to war and their fingers to fight,
Be able to put British armies to flight.

And now, brave Americans, since it is so,
That we are independent, we'll have them to know,
That united we are and united we'll be,
And from all British tyrants we'll try to keep free.

May heaven smile on us in all our endeavors,
Safeguard our seaports, our towns and our rivers
Keep us from invaders by land and by sea,
And from all who deprive us of our liberty.

But mostly the songs were crudely fashioned out of the experience of semi-educated farm boys. One such anonymous lad was stationed with Major General Benjamin Lincoln's army near Bound Brook, New Jersey during March 1777. The rebel soldiers were in winter quarters, holding down an outpost only seven miles from British and Hessian troops near New Brunswick. A month later, they were attacked in a memorable engagement. But in March, the anonymous soldier, presumably a New Jersey militiaman, sat down and wrote out the "Song of the Minute Man," which eventually found its way onto a broadsheet of the period. While the Minute Men were generally thought of as Massachusetts militia who trained themselves to fight the British in the period before the outbreak of hostilities, many state militias called themselves by the same name throughout the war.

Song Of The Minute Man[13]

Tune: "The Girl I Left Behind Me"

Come rise up brother Minute Men and let us have a chorus,
The braver and the bolder, the more they will adore us;
Our country calls for swords and balls and drums aloud doth rattle,
Our fifers' charms arise to arms, Liberty calls to battle.

We have some noble congressmen elected for our nurses,
And every jolly farmer will assist us with their purses;
We let them stay at home, we say, enjoy their wives with pleasure,
And we will go and fight our foes and save their lives and treasure.

Now to our station, let us march, and rendezvous with pleasure,
We have been like brave Minute Men to serve so great a treasure;
We let them see immediately that we are men of mettle,
We Jersey boys that fear no noise will never flinch for battle.

And when we do return again, it will be with glory,
For them that do remain at home to hear a valiant story;
They will draw near and [be] glad to hear, no doubting of the wonder,
That Minute Men, though one to ten, should bring the Tories under.

So let us not be dismayed although the Tories thunder,
They only want to ruin us and live upon our plunder.
Our cause is just, therefore we must withstand all their boodle,
If they advance, we will make them dance the tune of Yankee Doodle.

For most of the colonists, rebellion and armed conflict against established authority did not come easy. But for the growing number of Americans of Irish descent, revolt against the English was as natural as breathing. And so Irish tunes steadily infiltrated the rebel ranks, providing a strain of beautifully plaintive melodies and a familiarity with both oppression and resistance which stood the colonists in good stead.

One favorite with both the men who fought and their wives and sweethearts at home derived from the old Gaelic song, "Shule Aroon." The song dates back to the late seventeenth century when, after the Treaty of Limerick (1691), many Irish patriots enlisted in the French Army to fight against the English. One verse from that period goes:

Now my love has gone to France,
To try his fortune to advance,
If he e'er come back, 'tis but a chance....

During the French and Indian War, the Irish adapted the song to the battles of North America in which Irish youth drafted into the British Army were fighting. As the Revolution progressed, many an American family sang the familiar strains as they bid tearful farewells to their respective Johnnies off to fight for independence.

Johnny Has Gone For A Soldier

Tune: "Shule Aroon"

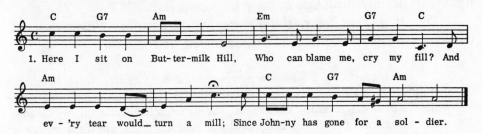

1. Here I sit on But-ter-milk Hill, Who can blame me, cry my fill? And ev-'ry tear would turn a mill; Since John-ny has gone for a sol-dier.

Me, oh my, I loved him so,
Broke my heart to see him go,
And only time will heal my woe,
Johnny has gone for a soldier.

I'll sell my rod, I'll sell my reel,
Likewise I'll sell my spinning wheel,
And buy my love a sword of steel,
Johnny has gone for a soldier.

I'll dye my dress, I'll dye it red,
And through the streets I'll beg for bread,
For the lad that I love from me has fled,
Johnny has gone for a soldier.

But of all the songs that Yankee Doodle took delight in, none were more popular than those that mocked the British Army and commented with derision on their military efforts. The scorn with which the British military first approached the colonists' efforts in the war, while considerably mellowed after Lexington, Concord, Bunker Hill and other engagements, nevertheless persisted throughout the war. As with imperial armies in other times, the British simply found it next to impossible to accept the fact that a ragged group of patriots, fighting on their own soil, ill-equipped and not trained in the traditional arts of warfare, could prove a match for the might of the strongest military machine then known to history.

After General Gage's ill-fated foray against the rebels at Lexington and Concord and the costly "victory" at Bunker Hill, the British retreated into the town of Boston while the newly formed American army laid siege to the port. Before the events of the spring of '75, the British used Boston as a base from which they could, at least, make a show of controlling Massachusetts. Afterwards, they were bottled up, unable to do anything but occupy the town itself.

Almost a year later, the *Pennsylvania Evening Post*, under a March 17 Massachusetts dateline, reported as follows:

> This morning the British army in Boston, under General Howe, consisting of upwards of 7,000 men, after suffering an ignominious blockade for many months past, disgracefully quitted all their strongholds in Boston and Charlestown, fled from before the army of the United Colonies, and took refuge on board their ships. . . . and with such silence and precaution did they embark that a great part of the inhabitants did not know it until after they were gone. . . . The joy of our friends in Boston, on seeing the victorious and gallant troops of their country enter the town almost at the heels of their barbarous oppressors, was inexpressibly great. The mutual congratulations and tender embraces which soon afterwards took place, between those of the nearest connections in life, for a long time cruelly rent asunder by the tyranny of our implacable enemies, surpasses description.

In the same issue of the *Pennsylvania Post*, and presumably to commemorate the occasion described above in appropriate fashion, appeared the following by Benjamin Franklin.

The King's Own Regulars

Words: Benjamin Franklin
Tune: "Villikins and His Dinah" [14]

Since you all will have singing and won't be said nay,
I cannot refuse when you so beg and pray;
So, I'll sing you a song, as a body may say,
'Tis of the king's regulars, who ne'er ran away.
    Oh, the old soldiers of the king,
    And the king's own regulars.

At Prestonpans [15] we met with some rebels one day,
We marshalled ourselves all in comely array;
Our hearts were all stout and bid our legs stay,
But our feet were wrong-headed and took us away.
    Oh, the old soldiers, etc.

No troops perform better than we at reviews,
We march and we wheel and whatever you choose;
George would see how we fight, and we never refuse,
There we all fight with courage—you may see't in the News.
    Oh, the old soldiers, etc.

It was not fair to shoot at us from behind trees:
If they had stood open (*spoken:* as they ought before our
    great guns), we'd have beat them with ease;
They may fight one another that way if they please,
But it is not regular to stand and fight with such rascals
    as these
    Oh, the old soldiers, etc.

At Fort George and Oswego, to our great reputation,
We showed our vast skill in fortification;
The French fired three guns, of the fourth they had no occasion,
For we gave up those forts—not through fear, but
    persuasion.
    Oh, the old soldiers, etc.

To Ticonderoga we went in a passion,
Swearing revenge on all the French nation;
But we soon turned tail without hesitation,
Because they fought behind trees, which is not the regular fashion.
    Oh, the old soldiers, etc.

Grown proud at reviews, great George had no rest;
Each grandsire, he'd heard, had a rebellion suppressed.
He wished a rebellion looked around and saw none,
So resolved a rebellion to make—of his own.
    Oh, the old soldiers, etc.

Our general with his council of war did advise
How at Lexington we might the Yankees surprise;
We marched and remarched, all surprised at being beat,
And that's how the plan of surprise was complete.
    Oh, the old soldiers, etc.

For fifteen miles they followed and pelted us, we scarce had time to pull a trigger,
But did you ever know a retreat performed with more vigor?
For we did it in two hours which saved us from perdition;
'Twas not in going out, but in returning, consisted our expedition.
    Oh, the old soldiers, etc.

Says our general, "We were forced to take to our arms in
    our own defense,"
(For *arms*, read *legs*, and it will be both truth and sense),
"Lord Percy,[16] (says he), I must say something in civility,
And that is, I can never enough praise him for his great
    agility."
    Oh, the old soldiers, etc.

Of their firing from behind fences he makes a great pother,
Every fence has two sides: they made use of one, and we only
    forgot to use the other.
That we turned our backs and ran away so fast, don't let
    that disgrace us,
'Twas only to make good what Sandwich[17] said, that the
    Yankees could not face us.
    Oh, the old soldiers, etc.

As they could not get before us, how could they look us in
    the face?
We took care they shouldn't by scampering away apace.
That they had not much to brag of is a very plain case,
For if they beat us in the fight, we beat them in
    the race.
    Oh, the old soldiers, etc.

In the early years of the war, the rebel victories were few and far between. The most successful engagements were those in which the British nominally succeeded, such as Bunker Hill, only to find that their "victory" was so dearly paid for that it amounted to a rebel success.

One early battle in which the colonists bested King George's men took place June 29, 1776 in Charleston harbor, South Carolina. Here, Sir Peter Parker, Admiral of the British fleet, led a naval assault on Sullivan's Island while an army led by Sir Henry Clinton massed for a land attack. But Clinton's troops held back, and Parker's attempt to storm the island by sea was beaten back by rebel forces under the command of General Charles Lee. In the course of the engagement, Admiral Parker's pants were shot away, an incident which gave the entire affair an outrageous aspect one Yankee songmaker proceeded to exploit in the form of a first-person account from the point of view of the unfortunate Sir Peter.

Sir Peter Parker [18]

With much labor and toil,
Unto Sullivan's Isle,
I came firm as Falstaff or Pistol,
But the Yankees, God rot 'em,
I could not get at 'em,
Most terribly mauled my poor Bristol. [19]

91

Bold Clinton by land
Did quietly stand,
While I made a thundering clatter;
But the channel was deep,
So he only could peep,
And not venture over the water.

Devil take 'em, their shot
Came so swift and so hot,
And the cowardly dogs stood so stiff, sirs!
That I put ship about,
And was glad to get out,
Or they would not have left me a skiff, sirs!

Now bold as a Turk,
I proceed to New York,
Where with Clinton and Howe you may find me.
I've the wind in my tail,
And am hoisting my sail,
To leave Sullivan's Island behind me.

But my lords, do not fear,
For before the next year,
Although a small island could fret us,
The Continent whole
We shall take, by my soul,
If the cowardly Yankees will let us.

Of all the rebel songs that poked fun at the British, none was more uproarious than Francis Hopkinson's "Battle of the Kegs." The song grew out of an inspired failure by the colonists to sink the British fleet stationed in the Delaware in January of 1778. David Bushnell, the inventor of the submarine, was a Yankee partisan whose experiments with undersea naval warfare, while practical, never succeeded in sinking a British warship.

When the British won control of the Delaware River, Bushnell hit on the idea of floating incendiary mines in the form of kegs of powder into the heart of the fleet. The plan failed, but its very attempt caused panic among the British. A contemporary newspaper account of the incident captures the flavor of the moment:

This city (Philadelphia) hath lately been entertained with an exhibition of most astounding activity, bravery and military skill of the royal army and navy of Great Britain. Some time last week, a keg of singular construction was seen floating down the river; the crew of a barge, attempting to take it up, it suddenly exploded with serious results to the crew. Last Monday some kegs of similar construction were seen and filled the royal troops with unspeakable consternation. It was reported that the kegs were filled with armed men, and that the points of the bayonets could be seen sticking from the bung-holes. The British ships of war were immediately manned. Hostilities were commenced without ceremony and incessant firing was poured upon the inoffensive kegs. Every chip or stick that floated by was a target for the vigor of the British arms. The action commenced about sunrise and lasted until noon, when the kegs were, as it were, put to flight; but just at this time a marketwoman let fall from a boat-load of provisions a keg of butter, which innocently floated down to the field of battle. At this supposed re-enforcement the attack was renewed, and the firing from the marine and land forces was beyond imagination, and continued until night closed the conflict. The British withdrew and celebrated the occasion as a great victory, receiving congratulations for their bravery and valor!

—New Jersey Gazette, January 9, 1778

Francis Hopkinson, a member of the Continental Congress from New Jersey, a signer of the Declaration of Independence and one of the Revolution's most distinguished figures, seized upon the incident to compose his famous ballad. The song was a roaring success with soldiers and civilians alike.

The Battle Of The Kegs [20]

Words: Francis Hopkinson
Tune: "Yankee Doodle"

Gallants attend, and hear a friend
Trill forth harmonious ditty,
Strange things I'll tell, which late befell,
In Philadelphia city.
'Twas early day, as poets say,
Just when the sun was rising,
A soldier stood on a log of wood
And saw a thing surprising.

As in amaze he stood to gaze,
The truth can't be denied, sir,
He spied a score of kegs or more
Come floating down the tide, sir.
A sailor, too, in jerkin blue,
This strange appearance viewing,
First damned his eyes in great surprise,
Then said, "Some mischief's brewing."

These kegs now hold the rebels bold,
Packed up like pickled herring,
And they're come down t'attack the town
In this new way of ferrying.
The soldier flew, the sailor, too,
And scared almost to death, sir,
Wore out their shoes to spread the news,
And ran till out of breath, sir.

Now up and down, throughout the town,
Most frantic scenes were acted,
And some ran here and others there,
Like men almost distracted.
Some fire cried, which some denied,
But said the earth had quakéd;
And girls and boys, with hideous noise,
Ran through the streets half naked.

Sir William[21] he, snug as a flea,
Lay all this time a-snoring,
Nor dreamed of harm as he lay warm
In bed with Mrs. Loring.[22]
Now in a fright, he starts upright,
Awaked by such a clatter,
He rubs his eyes and boldly cries,
"For God's sake, what's the matter?"

At his bedside, he then espied
Sir Erskine[23] at command, sir,
Upon one foot, he had one boot,
And t'other in his hand, sir.
"Arise! arise!" Sir Erskine cries,
"The rebels—more's the pity—
Without a boat, are all afloat,
And ranged before the city.

"The motley crew in vessels new,
With Satan for their guide, sir,
Packed up in bags, or wooden kegs,
Come driving down the tide, sir.
Therefore prepare for bloody war,
These kegs must all be routed,
Or surely we despised shall be,
And British courage doubted."

The royal band now ready stand,
All ranged in dread array, sir,
With stomachs stout to see it out,
And make a bloody day, sir.
The cannons roar from shore to shore,
The small arms make a rattle;
Since wars began, I'm sure no man
E'er saw so strange a battle.

The rebel dales, the rebel vales,
With rebel trees surrounded,
The distant woods, the hills and floods,
With rebel echoes sounded.
The fish below swam to and fro,
Attacked from every quarter;
Why sure, thought they, the devil's to pay
'Mongst folks above the water.

The kegs, 'tis said, though strongly made
Of rebel staves and hoops, sir,
Could not oppose their powerful foes,
The conquering British troops, sir.
From morn till night, these men of might
Displayed amazing courage;
And when the sun was fairly down,
Retired to sup their porridge.

An hundred men, with each a pen,
Or more, upon my word, sir,
It is most true would be too few,
Their valor to record, sir.
Such feats did they perform that day
Against those wicked kegs, sir,
That years to come, if they get home,
They'll make their boasts and brags, sir.

Another popular composition of Hopkinson was the following tribute to George Washington, written about the same time as "The Battle of the Kegs."

A Toast [24]

Words and music: Francis Hopkinson

1. 'Tis Wash-ing-ton's health, fill a bump-er a - round, For— he is our glo - ry and pride; Our— arms shall in bat - tle with con-quest be crowned,—Whilst vir - tue and he's— on our side. Our— arms shall in bat - tle with con-quest be crowned—Whilst vir - tue and he's— on our side,—And— he's—— on our side.

'Tis Washington's health loud cannons should roar,
And trumpets the truth should proclaim;
There cannot be found, search all the world o'er,
His equal in virtue and fame, etc.

'Tis Washington's health our hero to bless,
May heaven look graciously down;
Oh! long may he live, our hearts to possess,
And freedom still call him her own, etc.

Washington, of course, was the focus for a number of songs of the period, most of them invoking his virtues, as did Hopkinson's, with elaborate literary flourishes. Historians of later years suggest that some of these were "enormously popular," but one wonders whether such estimates may not have been inflated by a certain euphoric historiography common to mid-nineteenth-century writers.

Perhaps the most popular of the Washington songs was this

composition by Jonathan Sewall, who also wrote "On Independence" (q.v.).

War And Washington[25]

Words: Jonathan Mitchell Sewall
Tune: "The British Grenadiers"

Vain Britons, boast no longer, with proud indignity,[26]
By land your conquering legions, your matchless strength at sea,
Since we, your braver sons incensed, our swords have girded on,
Huzza, huzza, huzza, huzza, for war and Washington.

Urged on by North and vengeance, those valiant champions came,
Loud bellowing "Tea and Treason," and George was all on flame;
Yet sacrilegious as it seems, we rebels still live on,
And laugh at all their empty puffs, huzza for Washington!

Great heavens! Is this the nation whose thundering arms were hurled
Through Europe, Africa, India? Whose navy ruled a world?
The lustre of your former deeds, whole ages of renown,
Lost in a moment, or transferred to us and Washington!

Yet think not thirst of glory unsheaths our vengeful swords
To rend your bands asunder, or cast away your cords,
'Tis heaven-born freedom fires us all, and strengthens each brave son,
For him who humbly guides the plough to god-like Washington.

Should warlike weapons fail us, disdaining slavish fears,
To swords we'll beat our ploughshares, our pruning-hooks to spears,
And rush, all desperate, on our foe, nor breathe till battle won,
Then shout, and shout America! and conquering Washington!

But there were other heroes as well; Paul Revere, who spread the alarm to Lexington and Concord; Joseph Warren, who died at Bunker Hill; Ethan Allen and General Montgomery; John Paul Jones and "Mad Anthony" Wayne, and countless others. Some were memorialized in song and others in legend and story.

Of those whose bravery inspired the rebel cause, none was more celebrated than a twenty-one-year-old captain from Connecticut by the name of Nathan Hale. A one-time schoolteacher, Hale volunteered for an intelligence mission during the New York campaign of 1776. He was captured by the British while returning to his own lines. Probably, he was betrayed by his cousin, Samuel Hale, General Howe's deputy commissioner of prisoners. Apparently he confessed immediately and was ordered summarily executed the following day by General Howe. Before being hanged on September 22, 1776, he is reported to have said, as his final words, "I only regret that I have but one life to lose for my country."

No one knows for sure when this ballad was written, although it is presumed to have been composed shortly after Hale's death.

Nathan Hale[27]

Cooling shades of the night were coming apace,
The tattoo had beat, the tattoo had beat.
The noble one sprang from his dark lurking place,
To make his retreat, to make his retreat.

He warily trod on the dry rustling leaves,
As he passed through the wood, as he passed through the wood;
And silently gained his rude launch on the shore,
As she played with the flood, as she played with the flood.

The guards of the camp on that dark, dreary night,
Had a murderous will, had a murderous will.
They took him and bore him afar from the shore,
To a hut on the hill, to a hut on the hill.

No mother was there, nor a friend who could cheer,
In that little stone cell, in that little stone cell.
But he trusted in love from his father above,
In his heart, all was well, in his heart, all was well.

An ominous owl with his solemn bass voice,
Sat moaning hard by, sat moaning hard by.
"The tyrant's proud minions most gladly rejoice,
For he must soon die; for he must soon die."

They took him and bound him and bore him away,
Down the hill's grassy side, down the hill's grassy side.
'Twas there the base hirelings, in royal array,
His cause did deride, his cause did deride.

Five minutes were given, short moments, no more,
For him to repent, for him to repent;
He prayed for his mother, he asked not another,
To heaven he went, to heaven he went.

The faith of a martyr, the tragedy shewed,
As he trod the last stage, as he trod the last stage.
As Britons will shudder at gallant Hale's blood,
As his words do presage, as his words do presage.

Another much-sung hero of the Revolution was General "Mad Anthony" Wayne, whose victory at Stony Point in July 1779 was one of the most important of the war. A great inspirational figure, Wayne was widely admired as a fearless leader who took at least as many risks in battle as any of his men. His victory at Stony Point provided an enormous boost in morale for the beleaguered American forces and resulted in paralyzing British General Clinton's operations. The lyrics are attributed to one of Wayne's aides-de-camp.

Mad Anthony Wayne [28]

Words: Anonymous
Music: Albert G. Emerick

Allegro spiritoso

His sword-blade gleams, and his eye-light beams, And_ nev-er glanced ei-ther in

vain; Like the o - cean tides, at our head he rides, The_

fear-less Mad An-tho-ny Wayne! Bang! bang! the ri-fles go, Down falls the

star-tled foe; Bang! bang! the ri-fles go, Down falls the star-tled foe; And

many a red coat here to-night, The Con - ti - nen - tals scorn-ing, Shall

nev-er meet the blaze of the broad sun-light, That shines on the mor-row morn-ing. And

many a red coat here to-night, The Con - ti - nen - tals scorn-ing, Shall

nev-er meet the blaze of the broad sun-light, That shines on the mor-row morn-ing.

Was e'er a chief of his speech so brief,
Who utters his wishes so plain?
Ere he speaks a word, the orders are heard
From the eyes of Mad Anthony Wayne!
Aim! Fire! exclaim his eyes,
Bang! Bang! each gun replies.
Aim! Fire! exclaim his eyes,
Bang! Bang! each gun replies. *(Cho.)*

It is best to fall at our country's call,
If we must leave this lifetime of pain;
And who would shrink from the perilous brink
When led by Mad Anthony Wayne?
Ran! Tan! the bugles sound,
Our forces fill the ground.
Ran! Tan! the bugles sound,
Our forces fill the ground. *(Cho.)*

Let them form their ranks in firm phalanx,
It will melt at our rifle-ball rain,
Every shot must tell on a redcoat well,
Or we anger Mad Anthony Wayne.
Tramp! Tramp! away they go,
Now retreats the beaten foe.
Tramp! Tramp! away they go,
Now retreats the beaten foe. *(Cho.)*

Still another Yankee soldier who generated legends of his exploits was John Stark of New Hampshire. Distinguishing himself in the battle of Bunker Hill, he later administered a decisive defeat to General "Gentleman Johnny" Burgoyne at the famous battle of Bennington. He also played a key role in the crucial Battle of Saratoga, which finally routed the ill-fated Burgoyne expedition.

Riflemen of Bennington [29]

Words: Traditional
Music: John Allison

Why come ye hith-er, red-coats, your__ minds what mad-ness fills? In our
val-leys there is dan-ger, And there's dan-ger in our hills. Oh__
hear ye not the sing-ing Of the bu-gle wild and free? Full__
soon you'll know the ring-ing Of the ri-fle from the tree. For the ri-fle, (Clap..
....) For the ri-fle, (Clap.....) In our hands will prove no tri-fle.____

Ye ride a goodly steed,
Ye may know another master,
Ye forward come with speed,
But ye'll learn to back much faster.
When ye meet our mountain boys
And their leader, Johnny Stark,
Lads who make but little noise,
Lads who always hit the mark! *(Cho.)*

Had ye no graves at home
Across the briny water,
That hither ye must come
Like bullocks to the slaughter?
If we the work must do,
Why the sooner 'tis begun,
If flint and trigger hold but true,
The quicker 'twill be done. *(Cho.)*

No event of the Revolution produced greater consternation than the attempt by Benedict Arnold to betray the American fort at West Point. On the morning of September 26, 1780, General Greene announced to the Continental Army, in his general orders of the day:

> *Treason* of the blackest dye was yesterday discovered! General Arnold, who commanded at West Point, lost to every sentiment of honor, of public and private obligation, was about to deliver up that important post into the hands of the enemy. Such an event must have given the American cause a deadly wound if not a fatal stab. Happily, the treason has been timely discovered to prevent the fatal misfortune. The providential train of circumstances which led to it affords the most convincing proof that the liberties of America are the object of divine protection.

There is no need to recount the details of Arnold's treason here. The story is too well known and too widely documented to require repetition. One should note, however, that a goodly amount of hyperbole and mythology has grown up around the incident. For one thing, the assessment that the fall of West Point would have destroyed the rebel cause is no longer the common view. Most historians would now tend to agree with the appraisal of John Alden that "the fall of West Point to the British would by no means have brought an end to the war." As numerous military debacles demonstrated, the Revolution was not to be defeated by a single event, no matter how seemingly disastrous.

Part of the romantic legend surrounding Arnold's treason has to do with the "noble" spirit and character of the British agent in the scheme, Major John André, and the fidelity to the rebel cause of the three American militiamen who captured André. The sentimentalism surrounding André's fate has to do, naturally, with the fact that the Briton died serving his country while Arnold, the traitor, escaped.

John Paulding, one of the three militiamen who captured André, became the subject of a ballad that quickly became the most widely known popular account of the entire affair. Paulding, only twenty-two at the time, had but recently escaped from a British military prison. Paulding's party were "volunteer militiamen" who were operating under a recently enacted regulation permitting them to claim any property found on a captured enemy. Their primary interest in first stopping André, then, was undoubtedly the possibility of some very material gain.

Upon being stopped by Paulding and the others behind American lines, André thought that his captors were Tories. The militiamen played along with this in order to get André to reveal himself, which he subsequently did, saying "I am a British officer on business of importance and must not be detained."

The militiamen then took his watch and asked him for his money. At this point, André tried to switch sides, but his captors were more interested in loot than explanations and decided to search him. They found no money but did find the secret papers that André was carrying which revealed the entire plot. André is then reported to have offered the Americans a substantial bribe if they would return him to British lines, but the militiamen feared a trap and decided to turn their prisoner over to their commanding officer.

And so Arnold's plot was discovered and thwarted. The American general fled to the British lines, the unfortunate André was hung, and a legend was born.

The following ballad came into currency within a short time of the events.

Brave Paulding and the Spy [30]

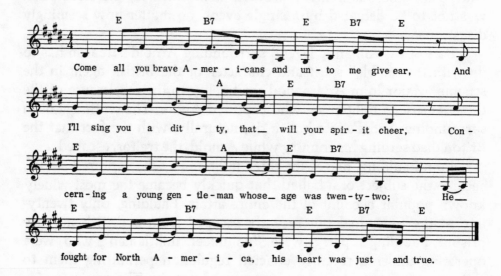

Come all you brave A-mer-i-cans and un-to me give ear, And I'll sing you a dit-ty, that will your spir-it cheer, Con-cern-ing a young gen-tle-man whose age was twen-ty-two; He fought for North A-mer-i-ca, his heart was just and true.

They took him from his dwelling and they did him confine,
They cast him into prison and kept him there a time.
But he with resolution resolved not long to stay;
He set himself at liberty and soon he ran away.

He with a scouting party went down to Tarrytown,
Where he met a British officer, a man of high reknown;
Who says unto these gentlemen, "You're of British cheer,
I trust that you can tell me if there's any danger near."

Then up stepped this young hero, John Paulding was his name,
"Sir, tell us where you're going, and also whence you came?"
"I bear the British flag, sir, I've a pass to go this way,
I'm on an expedition and have no time to stay."

Then round him came this company and bid him to dismount;
"Come, tell us where you're going, give us a strict account;
For we are now resolved that you shall ne'er pass by."
Upon examination, they found he was a spy.

He pleaded for his liberty, he begged for his discharge,
And oftentimes he told them, if they'd set him at large,
"Here's all the gold and silver I have laid up in store,
But when I reach the city, I'll give you ten times more."

"I want not the gold and silver you have laid up in store,
And when you get to New York, you need not send us more;
But you may take your sword in hand to gain your liberty,
And if that you do conquer me, oh then you shall be free."

"The time it is improper our valor for to try,
For if we take our swords in hand, then one of us must die;
I am a man of honor, with courage true and bold,
And I fear not the man of clay, although he's clothed in gold."

He saw that his conspiracy would soon be brought to light;
He begged for pen and paper, and asked leave to write
A line to General Arnold, to let him know his fate,
And beg for his assistance; but now it was too late.

When the news it came to Arnold, it put him in a fret,
He walked the room in trouble till tears his cheek did wet;
The story soon went through the camp, and also through the fort;
And he called for the Vulture and sailed for New York.

Now Arnold to New York is gone, a-fighting for his king,
And left poor Major André on the gallows for to swing;
When he was executed, he looked both meek and mild;
He looked upon the people and pleasantly he smiled.

It moved each eye with pity, caused every heart to bleed,
And everyone wished him released and Arnold in his stead.
He was a man of honor, in Britain he was born;
To die upon the gallows, most highly he did scorn.

A bumper to John Paulding! Now let your voices sound,
Fill up your flowing glasses and drink his health around;
Also to those young gentlemen who bore him company;
Success to North America, ye sons of liberty!

André himself was something of a poet and song writer. He wrote a long, satiric ballad, "The Cow Chace," commenting on General "Mad Anthony" Wayne's attack on a blockhouse near Fort Lee during the summer of 1780, and is also reported to have written a "lament" while awaiting execution, although its authenticity is in some doubt.

One fascinating aftermath of the Arnold affair was Washington's attempt to capture the traitor after he had gone over to the British. In October of 1780, Arnold undertook to raise a legion of Tories and deserters to be used in special operations against the rebel army. Washington ordered Major Henry ("Light-Horse Harry") Lee to find some volunteers who would try to bring Arnold back and learn whether or not any other American officers had been involved in the plot.

John Champe, a sergeant-major of cavalry was picked for the mission. The plan was for him to "desert" to the British and infiltrate the enemy ranks. The scheme worked well. Champe "deserted" on October 20, and a few days later was accepted by the British into Arnold's legion. The American made contact with his superiors and informed them he could find no evidence of treason by any others. An elaborate plot to abduct Arnold came within a shadow of success, but was thwarted when the legion departed New York for Virginia unexpectedly. Champe was forced to accompany Arnold to Virginia and only much later did he escape and return to Yankee lines. Until his return, none of Champe's comrades were aware of his secret mission. All had thought that his desertion was real and so the eventual revelation of the truth undoubtedly contributed to the legend of Sergeant Champe which the following song popularized.

Sergeant Champe [31]

Words: Anonymous
Tune: "Barbara Allen"

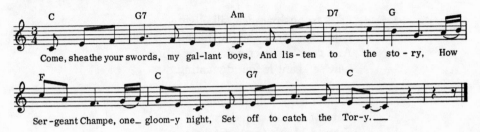

Come, sheathe your swords, my gal-lant boys, And lis-ten to the sto-ry, How
Ser-geant Champe, one_ gloom-y night, Set off to catch the Tor-y.__

You see, the general had got mad
To think his plans were thwarted,
And swore by all, both good and bad,
That Arnold should be carted.

So unto Lee he sent a line,
And told him all his sorrow,
And said that he must start the hunt
Before the coming morrow.

Lee found a sergeant in his camp
Made up of bone and muscle,
Who ne'er knew fear, and many a year
With Tories had a tussle.

Bold Champe, when mounted on old Rip,
All buttoned up from weather,
Sang out, "Goodbye!" cracked off his whip,
And soon was in the heather.

He galloped on towards Paulus Hook,
Improving every instant—
Until a patrol, wide awake,
Descried him in the distance.

On coming up, the guard called out
And asked him where he's going—
To which he answered with his spur,
And left him in the mowing.

107

The bushes passed him like the wind,
And pebbles flew asunder;
The guard was left far, far behind,
All mixed with mud and wonder.

Lee's troops paraded, all alive,
Although 'twas one the morning,
And counting o'er a dozen or more,
One sergeant is found wanting.

A little hero, full of spunk,
But not so full of judgment,
Pressed Major Lee to let him go,
With the bravest of his reg'ment.

Lee summoned Cornet Middleton,
Expresséd what was urgent,
And gave him orders how to go
To catch the rambling sergeant.

Then forty troopers, more or less,
Set off across the meader;
'Bout thirty-nine went jogging on
A-following their leader.

At early morn, a-down a hill,
They saw the sergeant sliding;
So fast he went, it was not ken't,
Whether he's rode, or riding.

None looked back, but on they spurred,
A-gaining every minute,
To see them go, 'twould done you good,
You'd thought old Satan in it.

The sergeant missed 'em, by good luck,
And took another tracing,
He turned his horse from Paulus Hook,
Elizabethtown facing.

It was the custom of Sir Hal[32]
To send his galleys cruising,
And so it happened just then
That two were at Van Deusen's.

Straight unto these the sergeant went,
And left old Rip, all standing,
A-waiting for the blown cornet,
At Squire Van Deusen's landing.

The troopers didn't gallop home,
But rested from their labors;
And some, 'tis said, took gingerbread
And cider from the neighbors.

'Twas just at eve the troopers reached
The camp they left that morning,
Champe's empty saddle, unto Lee,
Gave an unwelcome warning.

"If Champe has suffered, 'tis my fault,"
So thought the generous major,
"I would not have his garment touched
For millions on a wager!"

The cornet told him all he knew,
Excepting of the cider,
"The troopers all spurred very well,
But Champe was the best rider!"

And so it happened that brave Champe
Unto Sir Hal deserted,
Deceiving him, and you, and me,
And into [New] York was flirted.

He saw base Arnold in his camp,
Surrounded by the legion,
And told him of the recent prank
That threw him in that region.

Then Arnold grinned and rubbed his hands,
And e'enmost choked with pleasure,
Not thinking Champe was all the while
A-taking of his measure.

"Come now," says he, "my bold soldier,
As you're within our borders,
Let's drink our fill, old care to kill,
Tomorrow you'll have orders."

Full soon the British fleet set sail!
Say, wasn't that a pity?
Fur thus it was brave Sergeant Champe
Was taken from the city.

Base Arnold's head, by luck, was saved,
Poor André's was gobbeted,
Arnold's to blame for André's fame,
And André's to be pitied.

A revolutionary era tends to give rise to a widespread anti-authoritarian consciousness. While the American Revolution was primarily based upon a war for national independence from Britain, it encompassed far more profound revolutionary principles than national separation. And so it was that the revolt against authority engendered by the Revolution was not confined to the struggle against Britain but cropped up in internal divisions within the Colonies and the Continental Army itself. One of these conflicts arose from the class structure of the army. The petty privileges of the officers, the frequently gross disparity in provisions and accommodations, and the general authoritarian tone inherited from the limited military experience some of the American officers had had with the British Army all contributed to antagonisms within the Revolutionary ranks.

From time to time these conflicts erupted into serious explosions. In the later years of the war, especially as the three-year enlistment terms of many of the soldiers expired, mutinies in the ranks broke out with increasing frequency. The first of these took place January 1, 1780, when 100 soldiers of the Massachusetts Line marched off their posts determined to go home. They claimed that their term of enlistment had expired. The soldiers were pursued and brought back, and while a few were punished, most were pardoned immediately.

More serious was the mutiny of the Connecticut Line in May of that same year at Morristown, New Jersey. Here two regiments, after having gone without pay for five months and on short rations for several weeks, prepared to march off. A private involved in the affair described the soldiers "venting our spleen at our country and government, then at our officers, and then at ourselves for our imbecility in staying there and starving . . . for an ungrateful people who did not care what became of us."

Even more serious was the mutiny of the Pennsylvania Line which began on New Year's Day, 1781. Again, the accumulated grievances concerning food, clothing, quarters, pay, etc., together with claims that the terms of enlistment had expired, led to the uprising. The mutiny lasted for ten days and some 1,500 Continental troops were involved in it at its high point. Many of the mutineers planned a march on Philadelphia to confront the Congress with their demands. Washington and the generals were quite concerned about checking the possible spread of the mutiny throughout the army, since there was widespread sympathy for the rebels. The mutiny was finally negotiated to a settlement by leaders of the uprising and the officers, but another revolt, this from New Jersey troops, followed in its wake, as a sympathy action. Eventually, four of the New Jersey mutineers were executed.

No one knows for sure which of these mutinies, if any, gave rise to the following song. But it would be surprising if its anonymous author was not involved in one of them.

A New Song, Written by a Soldier [33]
Tune: Traditional

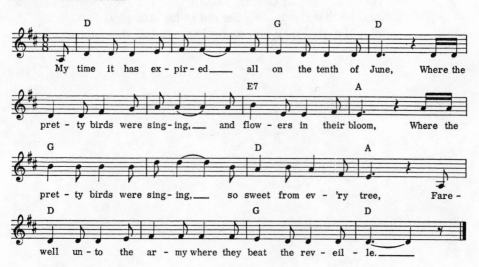

And to you my lovely officers, a word I have to say,
Before you go to battle, consider well I pray,
See how you kept our wages back, and robbed us of our clothes,
That we so dearly paid for in hard fatiguing blows.

And to you my lovely officers, those lines were written for,
I'd have you to pray for a short and moderate war,
Pray for the strength of Sampson and great King David slight,
For there's scarcely one to twenty of you that's courage
    enough to fight.

Hear a word unto our counsel, that rules through every state,
I pray be honest-hearted, for knavery I hate,
Try for once to do justice, be liberal and free,
Deal fairly with a soldier, and he'll deal fair with thee.

What think you of a soldier that fights for liberty,
Do you think he fights for money, or to set his country free?
I'd have you consider, and bear it on your mind,
Lest you should want their help again, it might be hard to find.

Our officers on the right of us, our country on the left,
Our enemy in front of us a-firing at our breasts,
The devil he comes up behind, and brings up the rear,
And a soldier that escapes them all has never need to fear.

My time it has expired, my song is at an end,
Here's a health to General Washington and every soldier's friend,
And he that cheats a soldier out of his little pay,
May the devil take him on his back, to hell with him straightway.

chapter IV

Battles of the Revolution

Songs from Bunker Hill to Yorktown

I t is reasonable to suppose that most of the military engagements of the American Revolution were noted in ballad form—at least by those who took part in them, if no one else. But it was not an age that took particular note of those frequently awkward, sometimes starkly beautiful creations made by foot soldiers, housewives and farm lads. And so most of these have been lost to posterity, although an occasional song of typically vague folk antecedents does survive into later times. To those rhymesters who had access to print, however, history has proven kinder. And so many a ballad has lasted more from the accident of publication than any other noticeable merit.

The "shot heard 'round the world" was fired on Lexington green, April 19, 1775. But the military struggle with Britain was really not joined until two months later when the Battle of Bunker Hill demonstrated to the crown's commanders that this was no passing colonial revolt they were dealing with, but a full-scale rebellion that would not easily be crushed. The nominal British "victory" in this critical battle has since been judged a significant setback, in much the same way that all "guerrilla" forces set far greater store by the amount of damage inflicted on the enemy than on actual territory captured.

British casualties were more than double that of the colonials. Particularly damaging to the British cause was the high rate of loss among their officers (19 killed, 70 wounded). It was a blow the British were to feel increasingly as hostilities went on. The following ballad is a firsthand account of the battle, and its last two lines are as pithy a literary statement as any couplet by Alexander Pope.

Ballad Of Bunker Hill[1]

The soldiers from town to the foot of the hill, In barges and rowboats, some great and some small, They pottered and dawdled and twaddled until We feared there would be no attack after all.

Let the foeman draw nigh till the white of his eye
Comes in range with your rifles, and then let it fly,
And show to Columbia, to Britain and fame,
How justice smiles awful when freemen take aim!

But when they got ready and all came along,
The way they marched up the hillside wasn't slow;
We were not a-feared and we welcomed 'em strong,
Held fire till the word and then laid the lads low.

But who shall declare the end of the affair,
At sundown there wasn't a man of us there;
We didn't depart till we'd given 'em some,
We used up our powder and had to go home!

Within days of the battle, broadsides were appearing in the streets of Boston celebrating the event and saluting the colonial militia which had acquitted itself so well. One fifteen-stanza account by Nathaniel Miles was set to music by a young man, recently graduated from Rhode Island College, who later became one of the most distinguished of the early American composers—Andrew Law.

The American Hero[2]

Words: Nathaniel Miles
Music: Andrew Law

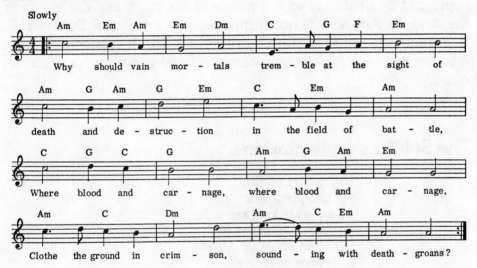

Now, Mars, I dare thee, clad in smoky pillars,
Bursting from bomb-shells, roaring from the cannon,
Rattling in grape-shot, rattling in grape-shot,
Like a storm of hailstones torturing Aether!

While all their hearts quick palpitate for havoc,
Let slip your bloodhounds, named the British lions,
Dauntless as death stares, dauntless as death stares,
Nimble as the whirlwind, dreadful as demons.

Still shall the banners of the King of heaven
Never advance where I'm afraid to follow;
While that precedes me, while that precedes me,
With an open bosom, war, I defy thee.

Fame and dear freedom lure me on to battle,
While a fell despot, grimmer than a death's head,
Stings me with serpents, stings me with serpents,
Fiercer than Medusa's to the encounter.

Life for my country, and the cause of freedom,
Is but a trifle for a worm to part with;
And if preserved, and if preserved
In so great a contest, life is redoubled.

The essential contradiction of all colonial wars is that soldiers of the imperialist army have little to die for, other than their mercenary's pay. In every colonial war the foot soldier of the imperial force is plagued by doubts as to the justice of his cause and the worth of the struggle. And so it is not surprising, in the wake of Bunker Hill, to encounter a song literature by dispirited British soldiers reflecting a bitterness towards their own command and a respect for the rebel cause.

The Soldier's Lamentation [3]

I am a jolly soldier,
Enlisted years ago,
To serve my king and country
Against the common foe.
But when across th' Atlantic
My orders were to go,
I grieved to think that English hearts
Should draw their swords on those
Who fought and conquered by their side
When Frenchmen were their foes.

'Twas on the seventeenth of June,
I can't forget the day,
The flower of our army
For Charlestown sailed away.
The town was soon in ashes laid,
When bombs began to play;
But oh! the cruel scene to paint,
It makes my blood run chill,
Pray heaven grant I never more
May climb up Bunker's Hill.

America to frighten,
The tools of power strove,
But ministers are cheated,
Their schemes abortive prove.
The men they told us would not fight
Are to the combat drove,
And to our gallant officers
It proved a bitter pill,
For numbers dropped before they reached
The top of Bunker's Hill.

I should not be amazed to hear
Wolfe's ghost had left the shades,
To check that shameful, bloody work,
Which England's crown degrades.
The lads who scorn to turn their backs
On Gallia's best brigades,
Undaunted stood, but frankly own
They better had lain still,
Than such a dear-bought vict'ry gain
As that of Bunker Hill.

Did they who bloody measures crave,
Our toil and danger share,
Not one to face the rifle-men,
A second time would dare.
Ye Britons who your country love,
Be this your ardent prayer:
To Britain and her colonies,
May peace be soon restored,
And knaves of high and low degree,
Be destined to the cord.

Shortly after Bunker Hill, with General Howe's forces tied down by the siege of Boston, the rebels undertook an invasion of Canada. It was a bold move, but ill fated. After victories at St. Johns on Lake Champlain and the capture of Montreal, the Americans came to grief before the walls of Quebec in a historic assault on New Year's Day.

Commanding the American forces was General Richard Montgomery, recently settled in the Colonies from Ireland with a distinguished military record earned while fighting on behalf of the crown. But when war broke out he enlisted under the colors of his new country. Montgomery's death at Quebec gave America her first war hero.

A Song On The Brave General Montgomery [4]

Words: Anonymous
Tune: Adaptation of "The Three Ravens" [5]

Come soldiers all in chorus join,
To pay the tribute at the shrine
 Of brave Montgomery,
Which to the memory is due
Of him who fought and died that you
 Might live and yet be free.

With cheerful and undaunted mind,
Domestic happiness resigned,
 He with a chosen band,
Through deserts wild, with fixed intent,
Canada for to conquer went,
 Or perish sword in hand.

Six weeks before St. John's they lay,
While cannon on them constant play,
 On cold and marshy ground;
When Prescott [6] forced at length to yield,
Aloud proclaimed it in the field,
 Virtue a friend had found.

To Montreal he winged his way,
Which seemed impatient to obey
 And opened wide its gates,
Convinced no force could e'er repel
Troops who had just behaved so well,
 Under so hard a fate.

With scarce one third part of his force
Then to Quebec he bent his course,
 That grave of heroes slain;
The pride of France, the great Montcalm,
And Wolfe, the strength of Britain's arm,
 Both fell on Abraham's plain.

Having no less of fame required,
There too Montgomery expired
    With Cheeseman [7] by his side.
Carleton,[8] 'tis said, his corpse conveyed
To earth in all the grand parade
    Of military pride.

The accident of historical preservation has given us a song about the British naval bombardment of the Rhode Island seaport town of Bristol in October 1775. In the long annals of the Revolution, the engagement was a minor one. A small British fleet, commanded by Captain James Wallace, appeared off Bristol on October 7 and demanded of the townspeople that they send a delegation to his ship to meet with him. The townspeople suggested that Wallace send his emissaries ashore, to which the British captain responded with a naval bombardment lasting an hour and a half. Convinced, a delegation went to meet with Wallace. To his initial demand for 200 sheep and 30 cattle—Wallace was on a foraging mission for the British fleet in Newport—the townspeople finally responded with 40 sheep, which apparently settled the matter, except for this ballad which has survived to re-create the moment.

The Bombardment Of Bristol [9]

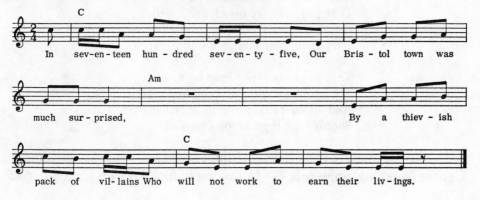

In sev-en-teen hun-dred sev-en-ty-five, Our Bris-tol town was much sur-prised, By a thiev-ish pack of vil-lains Who will not work to earn their liv-ings.

October, 'twas the seventh day,
As I have heard the people say,
Wallace—his name be ever cursed,
Came on our harbor just at dusk.

And there his ship did safely moor,
And quickly sent his barge ashore,
With orders that should not be broke,
Or that we might expect a smoke.

Demanding that our magistrates
Should quickly come on board his ship,
And let him have some sheep and cattle,
Or that they might expect a battle.

At eight o'clock by signal given,
Our peaceful atmosphere was riven;
Women with children in their arms,
With doleful cries ran to the farms.

With all their firing and their skill,
They did not any person kill,
Neither was any person hurt,
Except the Reverend Parson Burt.

And he was not killed by a ball,
As judged by jurors one and all,
But being in a sickly state,
He frightened fell, which proved his fate.

Another truth to you I'll tell,
That you may see they leveled well,
For aiming for to kill the people,
They fired their first shot into a steeple.

They fired low, they fired high,
The women scream, the children cry,
And all their firing and their racket
Shot off the topmast of a packet!

A young Irish officer, John Fitzgerald, an aide-de-camp to George Washington, wrote the following in his diary on December 25, 1776:

> Christmas morning. They make a great deal of Christmas in Germany, and no doubt the Hessians will drink a great deal of beer and have a dance tonight. They will be sleepy tomorrow morning. Washington will set the tune for them about daybreak. The rations are cooked. New flints and ammunition have been distributed.

Within a few short hours, the ragged rebel army sallied out of its winter quarters, slipped across the icy Delaware River, and surprised a 1,200-man Hessian force in the city of Trenton sleeping off its Christmas night celebration. Coming after a series of military reverses, the successful raid on Trenton electrified the Colonies and gave new hope to many whose revolutionary ardor had been waning in the long shadows of defeat. The Americans suffered a handful of casualties. By contrast, 106 Hessian mercenaries were either killed or wounded and more than 900 taken prisoner.

Many ballads recounting the events were assayed, including some Tory accounts which one collector found "too profane and corrupt for publication at the present time," leaving us to speculate on the literary extremes to which the American victory had driven the Loyalist poets. But this one was of Yankee making.

The Battle Of Trenton [10]

Words: Anonymous
Tune: Adaptation of "The Three Ravens"

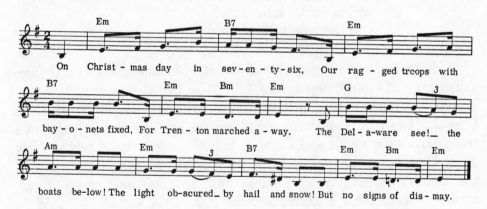

On Christ - mas day in sev - en - ty - six, Our rag - ged troops with bay - o - nets fixed, For Tren - ton marched a - way. The Del - a - ware see!— the boats be - low! The light ob - scured— by hail and snow! But no signs of dis - may.

Our object was the Hessian band,
That dared invade fair freedom's land,
    And quarter in that place.
Great Washington he led us on,
Whose streaming flag in storm or sun,
    Had never known disgrace.

In silent march we passed the night,
Each soldier panting for the fight,
   Though quite benumbed with frost.
Greene, on the left, at six began,
The right was led by Sullivan, [10a]
   Who ne'er a moment lost.

Their pickets stormed, the alarm was spread,
That rebels risen from the dead
   Were marching into town.
Some scampered here, some scampered there,
And some for action did prepare;
   But soon their arms laid down.

Twelve hundred servile miscreants,
With all their colors, guns and tents,
   Were trophies of the day.
The frolic o'er, the bright canteen,
In center, front and rear was seen
   Driving fatigue away.

Now, brothers of the patriot bands,
Let's sing deliverance from the hands
   Of arbitrary sway.
And as our life is but a span,
Let's touch the tankard while we can,
   In memory of that day.

The military turning point of the Revolution was General John Burgoyne's ill-fated campaign of 1777. The British commander's ambitious conception was a northern invasion of New York from Canada. The plan called for a linking up at Albany of Burgoyne's troops from the north and General Howe's forces, stationed in New York City, from the south. With full control of the Hudson River, the Colonies would be divided in half, supplies and troop movements between New England and the rest of the Colonies would be severely hampered, and the rebellion might well have been crushed.

But it was one of those strategies that always look better on paper than in practice. Imaginative harassment by the colonial militia created havoc in Burgoyne's army. At one point, the American general, Philip Schuyler, employed 1,000 axmen to fell trees across Burgoyne's path. Huge boulders were rolled into creeks and hastily dug ditches created swamp areas. At one crucial point in Burgoyne's campaign, it took him twenty days to cover twenty-two miles.

By the time Burgoyne reached Fort Edward, he was in a desperate situation. His supply lines from Montreal were overextended, the anticipated Tory uprising in the region failed to materialize, and the use of Indians against the civilian population angered both Burgoyne's own American supporters as well as those who supported the rebels. An expedition against Bennington, Vermont, in search of needed supplies, encountered the fierce resistance of Johnny Stark and his sharpshooters (see song, "Riflemen of Bennington") and resulted in a crushing defeat for the British. A daring raid on Fort Ticonderoga, captured by Burgoyne during his advance, posed a new threat to British supply lines and also provided the Americans with useful strategic information.

All of this culminated in the two battles of Saratoga (September 19 and October 7). Burgoyne's subsequent surrender on October 17 to General Gates brought the ambitious British scheme to an end in an unprecedented military disaster for the crown.

The exultation of the colonists knew no bounds. Ballads, broadsides, poems and songs detailing the historic battles were soon heard in the streets of Boston, Philadelphia, New York and Charleston. A ditty popular in Vermont at the time went:

> In seventeen hundred and seventy-seven,
> General Burgoyne set out for Heaven;
> But as the Yankees would rebel,
> He missed his route and went to Hell.

In London, one wit used the occasion to recount the failures of all the British commanders.

> Gage nothing did and went to pot;
> Howe lost one town, another got;
> Guy [11] nothing lost, and nothing won;
> Dunmore [12] was homewards forced to run;
> Clinton was beat and got a garter,
> And bouncing Burgoyne catched a Tartar;
> Thus all we gain for millions spent
> Is to be laughed at and repent.

The Burgoyne campaign was commemorated by many ballads. The two here were the best of the lot, the one from point of view of detail in the best of the ballad tradition, the other for its evocative imagery.

The Battle Of Saratoga[13]

Words: Anonymous
Tune: "Brennan on the Moor"[14]

Burgoyne, the king's commander, from Canada set sail,
With full eight thousand reg'lars, he thought he could not fail;
With Indians and Canadians and his curséd Tory crew,
On board his fleet of shipping, he up the Champlain flew.
    He up the Champlain flew, he up the Champlain flew,
    On board his fleet of shipping, he up the Champlain flew.

Before Ticonderoga, the first day of July,
Appeared his ships and army, and we did them espy.
Their motions we observéd full well both night and day,
And our brave boys preparéd to have a bloody fray.
    To have a bloody fray, etc.

124

Our garrison they viewed them, and straight their troops did land,
And when St. Clair, [15] our chieftain, the fact did understand,
That they the Mount Defiance were bent to fortify,
He found we must surrender or else prepare to die.
   Or else prepare to die, etc.

The fifth day of July, then, he ordered a retreat,
And when next morn we started, Burgoyne thought we were beat.
And closely he pursued us, till when near Hubbardton
Our rear guards were defeated, he thought the country won.
   He thought the country won, etc.

And when 'twas told in Congress that we our forts had left,
To Albany retreated, of all the north bereft;
Brave General Gates [16] they sent us, our fortunes to retrieve,
And him with shouts of gladness, the army did receive.
   The army did receive, etc.

Where first the Mohawk's waters do in the sunshine play,
For Herkimer's [17] brave soldiers, Sellinger [18] ambushed lay;
And them he there defeated, but soon he had his due,
And scared by Brooks [19] and Arnold, [20] he to the north withdrew.

To take the stores and cattle that we had gathered then,
Burgoyne sent a detachment of fifteen hundred men;
By Baum [21] they were commanded, to Bennington they went;
To plunder and to murder was fully their intent.

But little did they know then with whom they had to deal,
It was not quite so easy our stores and stock to steal;
Bold Stark [22] would give them only a portion of his lead;
With half his crew ere sunset, Baum lay among the dead.

The nineteenth of September, the morning cool and clear,
Brave Gates rode through our army, each soldier's heart to cheer;
"Burgoyne," he cried, "advances, but we will never fly;
No, rather than surrender, we'll fight him till we die."

The news was quickly brought us the enemy was near,
And all along our lines then there was no sign of fear;
It was above Stillwater we met at noon that day,
And everyone expected to see a bloody fray.

Six hours the battle lasted, each heart was true as gold,
The British fought like lions, and we like Yankees bold;
The leaves with blood were crimson, and then brave Gates did cry—
"'Tis diamond now cut diamond! We'll beat them, boys, or die."

The darkness soon approaching, it forced us to retreat
Into our lines till morning, which made them think us beat;
But ere the sun was risen, they saw before their eyes,
Us ready to engage them, which did them much surprise.

Of fighting they seem weary, therefore to work they go,
Their thousand dead to bury and breastworks up to throw;
With grape and bombs intending our army to destroy,
Or from our works our forces by stratagem decoy.

The seventh day of October, the British tried again,
Shells from their cannon throwing, which fell on us like rain;
To drive us from our stations, that they might thus retreat;
For now Burgoyne saw plainly, he never could us beat.

But vain was his endeavor our men to terrify;
Though death was all around us, not one of us would fly.
But when an hour we'd fought them and they began to yield,
Along our lines the cry ran, "The next blow wins the field!"

Great God, who guides their battles, whose cause is just and true,
Inspire our bold commander, the course he should pursue.
He ordered Arnold forward and Brooks to follow on;
The enemy was routed, our liberty was won!

Then burning all their luggage, they fled with haste and fear,
Burgoyne with all his forces, to Saratoga did steer;
And Gates, our brave commander, soon after him did hie,
Resolving he would take them or in the effort die.

As we came nigh the village, we overtook the foe,
They'd burned each house to ashes, like all where'er they go.
The seventeenth of October, they did capitulate,
Burgoyne and his proud army did we our pris'ners make.

Now, here's a health to Arnold and our commander Gates,
To Lincoln [23] and to Washington, whom every Tory hates;
Likewise unto our Congress, God grant it long to reign;
Our country, Right and Justice forever to maintain.

Now finished is my story, my song is at an end;
The freedom we're enjoying we're ready to defend;
For while our cause is righteous, heaven nerves the soldier's arm,
And vain is their endeavor who strive to do us harm.

The Fate Of John Burgoyne [24]

Words: Anonymous
Tune: "The Girl I Left Behind Me"

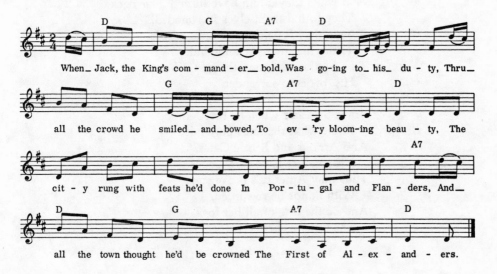

When_ Jack, the King's com - mand - er_ bold, Was go-ing to_ his_ du - ty, Thru_ all the crowd he smiled_ and_bowed, To ev - 'ry bloom-ing beau - ty, The cit - y rung with feats he'd done In Por - tu - gal and Flan - ders, And_ all the town thought he'd be crowned The First of Al - ex - and - ers.

To Hampton Court he first repairs,
    To kiss great George's hand, sirs,
Then to harangue on state affairs,
    Before he left the land, sirs.
The "lower house" sat mute as mouse,
    To hear his grand oration;
And "all the peers" with loudest cheers,
    Proclaimed him to the nation. [25]

Then off he went to Canada,
    Next to Ticonderoga,
And quitting those, away he goes,
    Straightway to Saratoga.
With great parade his march he made,
    To gain his wished for station,
When far and wide his minions hied,
    To spread his "Proclamation."

127

To such as stayed he offers made
Of "pardon on submission;
But savage bands should waste the lands
Of all in opposition."
But ah, the cruel fate of war!
This boasted son of Britain,
When mounting his triumphal car
With sudden fear was smitten.

The sons of freedom gathered round,
His hostile bands confounded,
And when they'd fain have turned their back,
They found themselves surrounded!
In vain they fought, in vain they fled,
Their chief humane and tender,
To save the rest, soon thought it best
His forces to surrender.

Brave St. Clair when he first retired,
Knew what the fates portended;
And Arnold and heroic Gates,
His conduct have defended.
Thus may America's brave sons
With honor be rewarded,
And be the fate of all her foes,
The same as here recorded.

An additional comment on Burgoyne's misfortunes was offered by Francis Hopkinson, whose *A Tory Medley*, written in 1780, contains the following lament:

Burgoyne's Disgrace [26]

Words: Francis Hopkinson
Tune: "God Save the King"

Burgoyne with thousands came
In hopes of wealth and fame,
What hath he done?
At Saratoga he
Had the disgrace to see
Each soldier manfully
Lay down his gun.

What shall we Tories do
If thus the rebel crew
   Rise whilst we fall?
Since they have France and Spain
To help their cause to gain,
Is not our strife in vain—
   Curse on them all!

Rebel triumphs were not confined to the land. Early in the war, Americans discovered they had a naval hero. His name was John Paul Jones, and as commander of the *Providence* and subsequently a small fleet, he scored sixteen victories on the high seas during 1776-77. Determined to bring the war to the British, Jones raided the English coast and even attempted to kidnap the Earl of Selkirk as a hostage in order to assure the safety of American prisoners.

The Scottish-born mariner was no amateur sailor. Apprenticed to a shipowner at the age of twelve, he subsequently found employment in the brisk slave trade and became first mate on a slaver at the age of nineteen. After winning a dubious reputation as a hard taskmaster aboard several vessels which he commanded in the West Indies, he added the Jones to his original name of John Paul and settled in the American colonies.

After his success with the *Providence*, Jones was given command of the sloop *Ranger*, which he took on a historic cruise in the Irish Sea in the spring of 1778 during which time he created havoc along the British coast. The following song celebrates this cruise.

The Yankee Man-of-War [27]

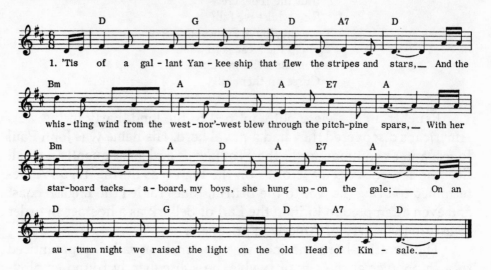

1. 'Tis of a gal-lant Yan-kee ship that flew the stripes and stars,— And the whis-tling wind from the west-nor'-west blew through the pitch-pine spars,— With her star-board tacks— a-board, my boys, she hung up-on the gale;—— On an au-tumn night we raised the light on the old Head of Kin-sale.——

It was a clear and cloudless night and the wind blew steady and strong,
As gaily over the sparkling deep our good ship bowled along;
With the foaming seas beneath her bow the fiery waves she spread,
And bending low her bosom of snow, she buried her lee cathead.

There was no talk of short'ning sail by him who walked the poop,
And under the press of her pond'rous jib, the boom bent like a hoop!
And the groaning waterways told the strain that held her stout main-tack,
But he only laughed as he glanced abaft at her white and foamy track.

The mid-tide meets in the channel waves that flow from shore to shore,
And the mist hung heavy upon the land from Featherstone to Dunmore;
And the sterling light in Tusker Rock where the old bell tolls each hour,
And the beacon light that shone so bright was quenched on Waterford Tower.

The nightly robes our good ship wore were her whole topsails three;
Her spanker and her standing jib—the courses being free,
"Now lay aloft, my heroes bold, not a moment must be passed,"
And royals and top-gallant sails were quickly on each mast.

What looms upon our starboard bow? What hangs upon the breeze?
'Tis time our good ship hauled her wind abreast the old Saltee's, [28]
For by her ponderous press of sail and by her consorts four,
We saw our morning visitor was a British man-of-war.

130

Up spake our noble captain then, as a shot ahead of us passed—
"Haul snug your flowing courses! Lay your topsail to the mast!"
Those Englishmen gave three loud hurrahs from the deck of their covered ark,
And we answered back by a solid broadside from the decks of our patriot bark.

"Out booms! out booms!" our skipper cried, "Out booms and give her sheet,"
And the swiftest keel that was ever launched shot ahead of the British fleet,
And amidst a thundering shower of shot with stun'sails hoisting away,
Down the North Channel Paul Jones did steer just at break of day.

John Paul Jones's most famous engagement took place September 23, 1779, when, commanding a small naval squadron, he encountered a British merchant fleet under convoy of the frigate *Serapis*, commanded by Captain Richard Pearson. Jones's ship was the *Bonhomme Richard*, its name deriving from the ship's French origin and the "Richard" a tribute to Benjamin Franklin's poor Richard. Jones's victory over Pearson was all the more remarkable because his ship was attacked not only by the *Serapis* but by one of the vessels in his own squadron, the *Alliance*, commanded by Pierre Landais, a half-crazed French ex-naval officer who was jealous of Jones. During the engagement the *Alliance* raked the *Bonhomme Richard* with three broadsides, one of which killed several members of Jones's crew. Jones's ship was so badly damaged in the battle that it sank two days later, but the captain's indomitable perseverance turned defeat into a brilliant triumph.

Many songs and ballads recounting the feats of the young naval hero followed the engagement. These songs came from both sides of the Atlantic. "Paul Jones' Victory" was originally an English broadside, written shortly after the historic battle, but it soon became popular also in America, where it drifted into folk tradition. Many versions of the ballad have been collected in both Canada and the United States.

Paul Jones' Victory[29]

Words: Anonymous
Tune: Traditional

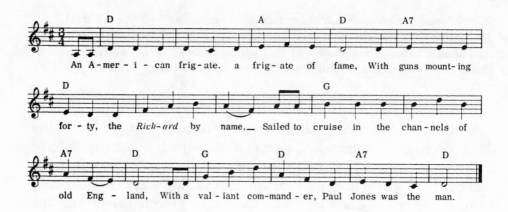

An A-mer-i-can frig-ate. a frig-ate of fame, With guns mount-ing for-ty, the *Rich-ard* by name,— Sailed to cruise in the chan-nels of old Eng-land, With a val-iant com-mand-er, Paul Jones was the man.

We had not cruised long before he espies
A large forty-four and twenty, likewise;
Well-manned with bold seamen, well laid in with stores,
In consort to drive us from old England's shores.

About twelve at noon Pearson came alongside,
With a loud-speaking trumpet, "Whence came you?" he cried;
"Return me an answer, I hailed you before,
Or if you do not, a broadside I'll pour."

Paul Jones then said to his men, everyone,
"Let every true seaman stand firm to his gun!
We'll receive a broadside from this bold Englishman,
And like true Yankee sailors, return it again."

The contest was bloody, both decks ran with gore
And the sea seemed to blaze while the cannon did roar;
"Fight on, my brave boys," then Paul Jones he cried,
"And soon we will humble this bold Englishman's pride."

"Stand firm to your quarters, your duty don't shun,
The first one that shrinks, through the body I'll run;
Though their force is superior, yet they shall know,
What true, brave American seamen can do."

The battle rolled on till bold Pearson cried:
"Have you yet struck your colors? Then come alongside!"
But so far from thinking that the battle was won
Brave Paul Jones replied, "I've not yet begun!"

We fought them eight glasses, eight glasses so hot,
Till seventy bold seamen lay dead on the spot,
And ninety brave seamen lay stretched in their gore,
While the pieces of cannon must fiercely did roar.

Our gunner in great fight to Captain Jones came,
"We gain water quite fast and our side's in a flame,"
Then Paul Jones said in the height of his pride,
"If we cannot do better, boys, sink alongside!"

The *Alliance* bore down and the *Richard* did rake
Which caused the bold hearts of our seamen to ache;
Our shot flew so hot that they could not stand us long,
And the undaunted Union of Britain came down.

To us they did strike and their colors hauled down,
The fame of Paul Jones to the world shall be known;
His name shall rank with the gallant and brave,
Whc fought like a hero our freedom to save.

Now all valiant seamen where'er you may be,
Who hear of this combat that's fought on the sea,
May you all do like them when called for the same,
And your names be enrolled on the pages of fame.

Your country will boast of her sons that are brave,
And to you she will look from all dangers to save;
She'll call you dear sons, in her annals you'll shine,
And the brows of the brave with green laurels entwine.

So now, my brave boys, have we taken a prize—
A large forty-four, and a twenty likewise.
Then God bless the mother whose doom is to weep
The loss of her sons in the ocean so deep.

A British ballad about John Paul Jones offers a remarkable view of England's internal conflicts at the time of the Revolution. With a tradition of bold seamanship behind them, the British couldn't help but admire the daring American captain's exploits.

One anonymous bard used the raids of the American sea captain to offer some pungent comments on the land pirates and incompetent ministers Britain was saddled with at the time. Among those pilloried in the song are George Sackville Germain, British secretary of state for the American colonies from 1775 to 1782, the Earl of Sandwich, first lord of the Admiralty (the "Jemmy Twicher" of the first verse), and Lord North, the prime minister.

Paul Jones[30]

Tune: "Little Mohee"

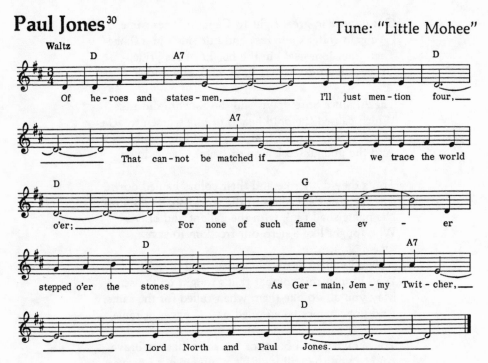

Of he-roes and states-men,_____ I'll just men-tion four,_____ That can-not be matched if_____ we trace the world o'er;_____ For none of such fame ev - er stepped o'er the stones_____ As Ger-main, Jem-my Twit-cher,_____ Lord North and Paul Jones._____

Through a mad-headed war which old England will rue,
At London, at Dublin, at Edinburgh, too,
The tradesman stands still, and the merchant bemoans
The losses he meets with from such as Paul Jones.

Contractors about this bold rebel harangue,
And swear, if they catch him, the traitor they'll hang;
But amongst these devourers of ten per cent loans [31]
Are full as great robbers as any Paul Jones.

Now happy for England would fortune but sweep
At once all her treacherous foes to the deep;
For the land under burdens most bitterly groans,
To get rid of some that are worse than Paul Jones.

To each jolly heart that is Britain's true friend,
In bumpers I'd freely this toast recommend:
"May Paul be converted, the Ministry purged,
Old England be free and her Enemies scourged."

From beginning to end, the American Revolution succeeded because the better-equipped British command consistently underestimated the rebel troops and tried to fight a pattern of classical war in an alien land.

No battle better demonstrates the fundamental flaw in the British scheme than the Revolution's final engagement at Yorktown, Virginia. General Charles Cornwallis was given the task of controlling the southern colonies of Georgia and South Carolina after the capture of Charleston in 1780. But eager to prove his own generalship, Cornwallis refused to play a passive role. A disastrous attack by General Horatio Gates (dazzled, perhaps, by his victory over Burgoyne at Saratoga) on the town of Camden, South Carolina led to a heady success for the Briton.

Cornwallis then undertook, largely on his own, a campaign into North Carolina and Virginia. Possibly he thought that such a bold military stroke could crush the rebellion once and for all. Ultimately, Cornwallis was trapped at Yorktown, Virginia, where after a thirteen day siege, he surrendered his entire army on October 19, 1781.

While George Washington commanded the last stages of this campaign, Cornwallis's downfall was largely the result of the dogged generalship of Nathanael Greene, who used guerrilla tactics to lead the British commander on a merry "dance" all across the Carolinas during 1780-81.

Cornwallis' Country Dance [32]

Tune: "Yankee Doodle"

Cornwallis led a country dance,
The like was never seen, sir,
Much retrograde and much advance,
And all with General Greene, sir.
They rambled up and rambled down,
Joined hands, then off they run, sir,
Our General Greene to Charlestown,
The earl to Wilmington, sir.

Greene, in the south, then danced a set,
And got a mighty name sir,
Cornwallis jigged with young Fayette [33]
But suffered in his fame, sir.
Then down he figured to the shore,
Most like a lordly dancer,
And on his courtly honor swore,
He would no more advance, sir.

Quoth he, my guards are weary grown,
With footing country dances,
They never at St. James's shone,
At capers, kicks, or prances.
Though men so gallant ne'er were seen,
While sauntering on parade, sir,
Or wriggling o'er the park's smooth green,
Or at a masquerade, sir.

Yet are red heels and long-laced skirts [34]
For stumps and briars meet, sir?
Or stand they chance with hunting-shirts,
Or hardy veteran feet, sir?
Now housed in York he challenged all,
At minuet or allemande,
And lessons for a courtly ball,
His guards by day and night conned.

This challenge known, full soon there came,
A set who had the bon ton,
De Grasse [35] and Rochambeau,[36] whose fame
Fut brillant pour un long temps.
And Washington, Columbia's son,
Whom easy nature taught, sir,
That grace which can't by pains be won,
Or Plutus' gold be bought, sir.

Now hand in hand they circle round,
This ever-dancing peer, sir;
Their gentle movements soon confound
The earl, as they draw near, sir.
His music soon forgets to play,
His feet can no more move, sir,
And all his bands now curse the day,
They jigged to our shore, sir.

Now Tories all, what can ye say?
Come—is not this a griper,
That while your hopes are danced away,
'Tis you must pay the piper.

Another Yankee account of the ill-fated Virginia campaign invented the most imaginative verb of the Revolution.

Cornwallis Burgoyned [37]

Tune: "Maggie Lauder"

When Brit-ish troops first land-ed here, With Howe com-mand-er o'er them, They thought they'd make us quake for fear, And car-ry all be-fore them; With thir-ty thou-sand men or more, And she with-out as-sis-tance, A-mer-i-ca must needs give o'er, And make no more re-sis-tance.

But Washington, her glorious son,
Of British hosts the terror,
Soon, by repeated overthrows,
Convinced them of their error;
Let Princeton and let Trenton tell
What gallant deeds he's done, sir,
And Monmouth's plains where hundreds fell,
And thousands more have run, sir.

Cornwallis, too, when he approached
Virginia's old dominion,
Thought he would soon her conqu'ror be,
And so was North's opinion.
From state to state with rapid stride,
His troops had marched before, sir,
Till quite elate with martial pride,
He thought all dangers o'er, sir.

But our allies, to his surprise,
The Chesapeake had entered;
And now too late, he cursed his fate,
And wished he ne'er had ventured.
For Washington no sooner knew
The visit he had paid her,
Than to his parent state he flew,
To crush the bold invader.

When he sat down before the town,
His Lordship soon surrendered;
His martial pride he laid aside,
And cased the British standard;
God! how this stroke will North provoke,
And all his thoughts confuse, sir,
And how the Peers will hang their ears,
When first they hear the news, sir.

Be peace, the glorious end of war,
By this event effected,
And be the name of Washington
To latest times respected;
Then let us toast America,
And France in union with her,
And may Great Britain rue the day
Her hostile bands came hither.

Although the terms of surrender were agreed to on October 17 and the formal capitulation took place on the nineteenth, it was not until early morning on October 22 that Philadelphia, where the Congress was sitting, got the news. An express rider from Governor Lee of Maryland came galloping into Philadelphia at two o'clock in the morning bearing a simple message from Admiral Count de Grasse for Thomas McKean, president of the Congress: "To be forwarded by night and day with the utmost dispatch—Lord Cornwallis surrendered the garrison of York to General Washington, the 17th October."

According to newspaper accounts of the day, "An honest old German, a watchman of Philadelphia, having conducted the express rider. . . to the door of his Excellency, the President of the Congress . . . continued the duties of his office, calling out: 'Basht dree o'glock, und Cornwallis isht da-ken!'"

Within a matter of days, broadsides were being peddled in the streets recounting, in ballad form, the wonderful news. The following is one of the best.

The Surrender Of Cornwallis [38]

Tune: "The British Grenadiers"

> Come all you bold Americans,
> The truth to you I'll tell,
> 'Tis of a sad misfortune
> Which late on Britain fell;
> 'Twas all in the heights of Yorktown,
> Where cannons loud did roar
> They summoned Lord Cornwallis
> To fight or else give o'er.
>
> A summons to surrender
> Was sent unto the Lord,
> Which made him feel like poor Burgoyne
> And quickly draw his sword,
> "Must I give o'er these glittering troops,
> These ships and Hessians, too,
> And yield to General Washington
> And his bold rebel crew?"
>
> A council to surrender,
> This lord did then command,
> "What say you, my brave heroes,
> To yield you must depend;
> For don't you see the bomb-shells fly,
> And cannons loud do roar,
> DeGrasse is in the harbor
> And Washington's on shore."

'Twas the nineteenth of October
In the year of eighty-one,
Cornwallis did surrender
To General Washington.
Six thousand chosen British troops
Marched out and grounded arms,
Huzza, ye bold Americans,
For now sweet music charms.

Six thousand chosen British troops
To Washington resigned,
Besides some ships and Hessians,
That could not stay behind;
With refugees and blackamores,
Oh, what a direful crew!
It was then he had some thousands,
But now he's got but few.

My Lord has gone unto New York,
Sir Harry [39] for to see;
For to send home this dreadful news
Unto his Majesty:
To contradict some former lines
Which he before had sent,
That he and his bold British troops
Would conquer where they went.

Here's a health to General Washington,
And his brave army, too,
And likewise to our worthy Greene,
To him much honor's due.
May we subdue those English troops
And clear the eastern shore,
That we may live in peace, my boys,
Whilst wars they are no more.

chapter V

For Good King George

Songs of Redcoats and Tories

As with all colonial armies, the songs of the British soldiers were basically nonideological. Unlike the Yankees, whose songs reflected the revolutionary energy of their cause, the British troops sang of drink, women and the vicissitudes of a soldier's life. Their most popular tunes—such as "British Grenadiers" and "The White Cockade"—had been a part of British military tradition for more than a century.

The melody for "The British Grenadiers" goes back to the sixteenth century, but the words which subsequently became more or less permanently enshrined in the tune date from 1690 during the struggle between James II and William of Orange.

The British Grenadiers [1]

Some talk of Alexander, and some of Hercules,
Of Hector and Lysander, and such great names as these;
But of all the world's brave heroes, there's none that can compare,
With a tow row row row row row, to the British Grenadier.

Whene'er we are commanded to storm the palisades,
Our leaders march with fuses, and we with hand grenades;
We throw them from the glacis about the enemies' ears,
Sing tow row row row row row, the British Grenadiers.

And when the siege is over, we do the town repair,
The townsmen cry, "Hurrah, boys, here comes a grenadier;
Here come the grenadiers, my boys, who know no doubts and fears,"
With a tow row row row row row to the British Grenadiers.

Then let us fill a bumper and drink a health to those
Who carry caps and pouches, and wear the louped clothes;
May they and their commanders live happy all their years,
With a tow row row row row row, for the British Grenadiers.

The supposedly carefree life of the soldier is a perennial theme of military songs. And in an age in which there was little security for a majority of the population, a life in the king's service surely had its appeals for the poverty-stricken. This one, a favorite of British troops who fought in the Revolution, is a classic of its genre.

How Happy The Soldier[2]

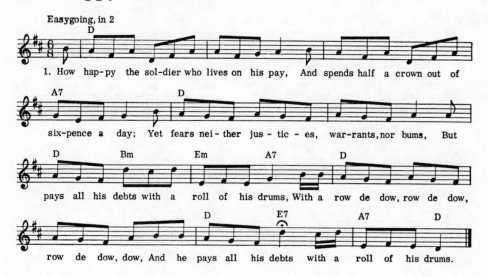

1. How hap-py the sol-dier who lives on his pay, And spends half a crown out of six-pence a day; Yet fears nei-ther jus-tic-es, war-rants, nor bums, But pays all his debts with a roll of his drums, With a row de dow, row de dow, row de dow, dow, And he pays all his debts with a roll of his drums.

He cares not a marvedy how the world goes,
His King finds his quarters and money and clothes;
He laughts at all sorrow whenever it comes,
And rattles away with the roll of his drums.
    With row de dow, row de dow, row de dow, dow,
    And he pays all his debts with the roll of his drums.

The drum is his glory, his joy and delight,
It leads him to pleasure as well as to fight;
No girl, when she hears it, though ever so glum,
But packs up her tatters and follows the drum.
    With row de dow, row de dow, row de dow, dow,
    She packs up her tatters and follows the drum.

Yet another song popular with the redcoats was a classic soldier's drinking tune, supposedly a favorite of Wolfe, who is reported to have ordered it sung the night before the Battle of Quebec in which he met his death. The song, known under a variety of titles including "The Duke of Benwick's March" and "Why, Soldiers, Why?", dates back to at least 1729 when it appeared in print for the first time. There is some evidence to suggest that rebel troops adopted the song and sang it with a great deal of bitterness, in the wake of military defeats, during the long winter camps.

How Stands The Glass Around[3]

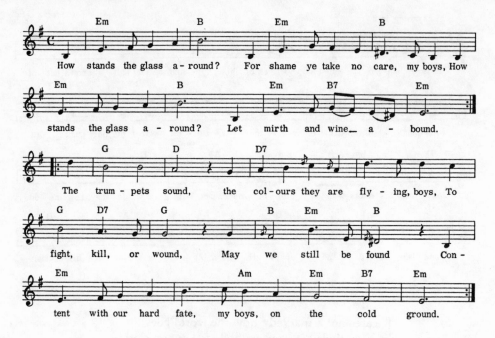

How stands the glass a-round? For shame ye take no care, my boys, How stands the glass a - round? Let mirth and wine_ a - bound.

The trum - pets sound, the col - ours they are fly - ing, boys, To fight, kill, or wound, May we still be found Con - tent with our hard fate, my boys, on the cold ground.

Why, soldiers, why,
Should we be melancholy, boys?
Why, soldiers, why,
Whose business 'tis to die!
What, sighing? Fie!
Damn fear, drink on, be jolly, boys,
'Tis he, you or I!
Cold, hot, wet or dry,
We're always bound to follow, boys,
And scorn to fly!

'Tis but in vain,
(I mean not to upbraid you, boys),
'Tis but in vain
For soldiers to complain.
Should next campaign
Send us to Him who made us, boys,
We're free from pain!
But if we remain,
A bottle and kind landlady
Cure all again.

A British soldier's song written during the war with the French in 1759 was revived by native Tories in the early years of the Revolution. The Loyalist publisher, James Rivington, printed this in his *New-York Gazetteer* of May 5, 1774, presumably as a bit of British braggadoccio by which the rebels might be warned of the foolhardiness of their cause. The song is the work of Edward Botwood, a sergeant in the Forty-seventh Grenadiers. It was written upon the embarkation of Botwood's regiment for Quebec with Wolfe. Botwood was killed in Wolfe's unsuccessful attempt to storm the French position at Montmorency Falls, July 31, 1759. A mid-nineteenth-century anthologist of Loyalist poetry found the last stanza of the piece a little too heady for his taste, so he eliminated it from his work, explaining that it was "clever but indecent."

Hot Stuff [4]

Words: Edward Botwood
Tune: "Lilies of France"

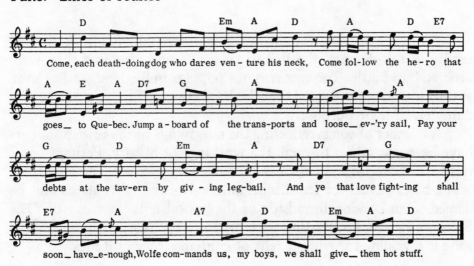

Up the river St. Lawrence our troops shall advance,
To "The Grenadier's March" we will teach them to dance.
Cape Breton we've taken and next we will try
At their capital to give them another black eye.
Vaudreil, [5] 'tis in vain you pretend to look gruff,
Those are coming who know how to give you Hot Stuff.

With powder in his periwig and snuff in his nose,
Monsieur will run down our descent to oppose;
And the Indians will come, but the Light Infantry
Will soon oblige them to take to a tree.
From such rascals as these may we fear a rebuff?
Advance, grenadiers, and let fly your Hot Stuff!

When the 47th Regiment is dashing ashore,
While bullets are whistling and cannons do roar,
Says Montcalm, "Those are Shirley's, [6] I know the lapels,"
"You lie," says Ned Botwood, "we belong to Lascelles! [7]"
Though our clothing is changed, yet we scorn a powder-puff;
So at you, ye bastards, here's give you Hot Stuff.

With Monckton [8] and Townshend, [9] those brave brigadiers,
I think we shall soon knock the town 'bout their ears.
And when we have done with the mortars and guns,
"If you please, Madam Abbess, a word with your nuns!"
Each soldier shall enter the convent in buff,
And then, never fear, we will give them Hot Stuff!

While the patriots fought out of political conviction or the necessity of self-defense, the British soldiers fought because they were
ordered into battle. The war was not popular in England, and as soon
as the king's troops learned that the Yankees could fight, many took a
dim view of their purpose.

A number of songs reflecting the misgivings of the British soldiers
have been passed on through the workings of history. Perhaps some
were artful propaganda devices of Yankee songwriters. But that there
was a basis in fact for the disenchantment of the redcoats cannot be
denied. One London broadside of the period tells the story of "The
Soldier's Farewell at Parting with his Wife for North America." The
song is revealing for what it tells of contemporary attitudes.

My orders I have received and them I must obey,
Against my will to go and fight in North America. . . .

When I went abroad before, 'twas with a valiant heart,
And ev'ryone wished me success when with me they did part.
But very few now wish success, alas! and well-a-day!
So what can I expect to meet in North America?

Many of the British troops were Irish draftees—as they were in virtually all of England's imperial wars. It is this aspect of English oppression of the Irish that has given rise to the vast literature of Irish antiwar songs from "Johnny I Hardly Knew Ye" to "The Minstrel Boy." One song filtered through the folk tradition helps to bring the time alive.

The Sons Of Liberty [10]

1. O fare you well, sweet Ireland, whom I shall see no more, My heart is almost bleeding to leave this native shore. The king he has commanded that we shall sail away To fight the boys of liberty in North America.

It was early in the morning, just at the break of day,
We hoisted British colors and anchored in Yorks Bay.
The sails a-being lassered they spread abroad to dry,
The Irish heroes landing, but the Lord knows who must die.

Through fields of blood we waded where the cannons loudly roar,
And many a galliant soldier lay a-bleeding in his gore,
And it's many a gallant commander, it's on the field did lay,
That was both killed and wounded by the Sons of Liberty.

Your hearts would have melted with pity to have seen the soldiers' wives,
A-hunting for their dead husbands and the melancholy cries,
And the children crying, "Mother, we surely rue the day
When we came for to lose our father dear in the North Amerikee."

Here's an end to my ditty, my song is at an end,
Here's a health to General Washington and all of his bold men,
God help a man protect him that is by land or sea,
For he had boys who feared no noise—the Sons of Liberty.

Closely related to the above is the ballad of "The Dying British Sergeant," which had currency as a broadside during the period of the Revolution. It appeared under various titles, including "The British Lamentation" and "General Gage." Some historians doubt the song's authenticity because of the last verse, although the sentiments expressed are not inconsistent with the disillusionment reflected in the rest of the song. It is also possible that the last stanza was added to the ballad later by a rebel rhymester.

The Dying British Sergeant [11]

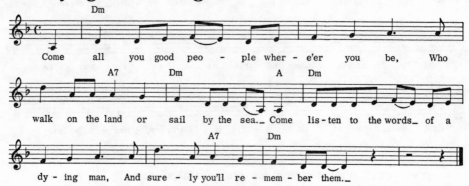

Come all you good peo—ple wher-e'er you be, Who walk on the land or sail by the sea. Come lis-ten to the words of a dy-ing man, And sure-ly you'll re-mem-ber them.

'Twas in December, the sixteenth day,
That we set sail for Amerikay,
Our drums and trumpets loud did sound,
And unto Boston we were bound.

And when to Boston we did come,
We thought by the aid of our British guns,
To make these Yankees own our king,
And daily tribute to him bring.

But to our sorrow and surprise,
We saw them, like grasshoppers, rise,
They fought like heroes in much rage
Which surely frightened General Gage.

Like lions roaring for their prey,
They feared no danger nor dismay;
True British blood runs through their veins,
And them, with courage, it sustains.

We saw those bold Columbia sons
Spread death and slaughter from their guns.
Freedom or death! was all their cry,
They did not seem to fear to die.

We sailed to York, sailed through the Sound,
And many a traitor there we found,
Who told us we could win the day—
There was no danger, they did say.

They told us 'twas a garden place,
And that our armies could, with ease,
Pull down their towns, lay waste their lands,
In spite of all their rebel bands.

A garden place it was indeed,
And in it grew many a bitter weed,
Which did pull down our highest hopes
And sorely wound the British troops.

'Tis now September, the seventeenth day,
I wish I'd ne'er come to America.
Full fifteen hundred have been slain,
Bold British heroes every one.

Now I've received my deathly wound,
I bid farewell to England's ground;
My wife and children will mourn for me,
Whilst I lie cold in Amerikee.

Fight on, America's noble sons,
Fear not Britannia's thundering guns.
Maintain your rights from year to year,
God's on your side, you need not fear.

Tories had their rhymesters, too, although how widely their
songs were sung would seem to be another case again. In the early
days of the rebellion, while the Colonists were still choosing sides,
Loyalist verses undoubtedly had wide currency. But as open warfare

broke out, one suspects that the Tory productions were largely confined to the few newspapers that, under the protection of the British occupation, would print them.

With New York in British hands for most of the war, the *Royal Gazette*, published by Rivington, was a prime outlet for these Tory songs. The two most active songsmiths in this regard were Jonathan Odell and Joseph Stansbury. The latter had only recently come to the shores of America in 1767, but Odell was descended from a family who had arrived in 1639. The songwriting pair did more than pillory the rebel cause with rhyme, however. The two became secret British agents and handled the correspondence between Benedict Arnold and John André, although this information did not become known until some time later.

Since both used various pseudonyms or else had their verses printed anonymously, it is not always an easy matter to ascribe appropriate accreditation. But it is safe to say that some of the songs which follow are of their making.

While the Continental Congress was meeting in 1776 and taking its first halting steps in the direction of uniting the rebellious Colonies, Tory songmakers lampooned their efforts. Here is a particularly biting comment.

The Congress [12]

Tune: "Nancy Dawson"

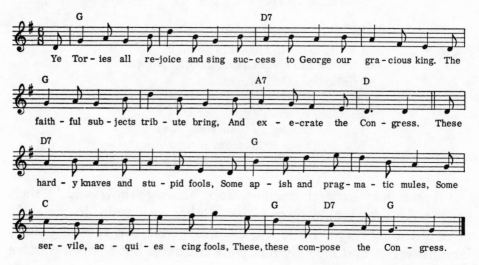

Ye Tor-ies all re-joice and sing suc-cess to George our gra-cious king. The faith-ful sub-jects trib-ute bring, And ex-e-crate the Con-gress. These hard-y knaves and stu-pid fools, Some ap-ish and prag-ma-tic mules, Some ser-vile, ac-qui-es-cing fools, These, these com-pose the Con-gress.

When Jove resolved to send a curse,
And all the woes of life rehearse,
Not plague, not famine, but much worse;
    He cursed us with a Congress

Then peace forsook this hapless shore,
Then cannons blazed with horrid roar;
We hear of blood, death, wounds and gore,
    The offspring of the Congress.

With freemen's rights they wanton play,
At their command, we fast and pray,
With worthless paper, they us pay,
    A fine device of Congress.

Time serving priests to zealots preach,
Who king and parliament impeach,
Seditious lessons us to teach
    At the command of Congress.

Good Lord! disperse this venal tribe,
Their doctrine let no fools imbibe,
Let Balaam no more asses ride
    Nor burdens bear to Congress.

Old Catiline, and Cromwell too,
Jack Cade and his seditious crew,
Hail brother rebel at first view,
    And hope to meet the Congress.

The world's amazed to see the pest,
The tranquil land with wars infest,
Britannia puts them to the test,
    And tries the strength of Congress.

Clinton, Burgoyne and gallant Howe,
Will soon reward our conduct true,
And to each traitor give his due,
    Perdition waits the Congress.

There's Washington and all his men—
Where Howe had one, the goose had ten—
Marches up the hill and down again,
    And sent returns to Congress.

Prepare, prepare, my friends prepare,
For scenes of blood, the field of war;
To royal standard we'll repair,
    And curse the haughty Congress.

Huzza! huzza! we thrice huzza!
Return peace, harmony and law!
Restore such times as once we saw
    And bid adieu to Congress.

A song which seems to have been popular with the Loyalists—
judging from the fact that it appears several times over in broadside
form—is this jibe which appeared early in the war. It was published
first in the *Halifax Journal*, suggesting that distance may have had
something to do with the author's daring.

The Burrowing Yankees [13]

Tune: "Villikins and His Dinah"

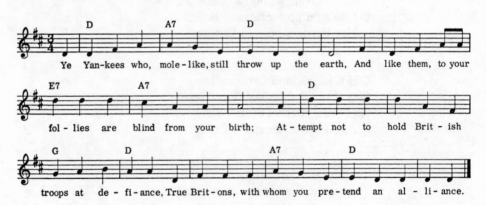

Ye Yan-kees who, mole-like, still throw up the earth, And like them, to your fol-lies are blind from your birth; At-tempt not to hold Brit-ish troops at de-fi-ance, True Brit-ons, with whom you pre-tend an al-li-ance.

Mistake not, such blood ne'er ran in your veins,
Tis no more than the dregs, the lees, or the drains;
Ye effect to talk big of your hourly attacks;
Come on! and I'll warrant, we'll soon see your backs.

Such threats of bravadoes serve only to warm
The true British hearts, you ne'er can alarm;
The Lion, once roused, will strike such a terror,
Shall show you, poor fools, your presumption and error.

And the time will soon come when your whole rebel race
Will be drove from the lands, nor dare show your face.
Here's a health to great George, may he fully determine
To root from the earth all such insolent vermin.

With the British occupying, at various times, Boston, New York and Philadelphia, Tory poets were eager to pay tribute to their protectors. Whether their object was to curry favor with the British military or to express deeply felt sentiments of loyalty ultimately makes little difference—and undoubtedly there was an element of both in these Tory compositions.

One of the most popular appeared in Rivington's *Royal Gazette* in 1778, with a note saying that the song, "though never yet published, has been frequently sung and re-echoed, in loyal companies, for many months past in this city."

The British Light Infantry [14]
Tune: "Black Sloven"

Though rebels unnumbered oppose their career,
Their hearts are undaunted, they're strangers to fear;
No obstacles hinder, resistless they go,
And death and destruction attend every blow.

'Cross the deep-gullied vale, up the mountain's steep side,
Through the rough foaming river's impetuous tide,
O'er the fortified redoubt, close wedged in array,
Regardless of safety they follow their prey.

The alarm of the drum and the cannon's loud roar,
The musket's quick flash, but inflames them the more.
No dangers appal, for they fear no control,
But glory and conquest inspires every soul.

Whenever their foe stands arranged in their sight,
With ardor impatient they pant for the fight;
Rout, havoc, confusion they spread, through the field,
And rebellion and treason are forced to yield.

Yankee military defeats were, of course, a perennial source of Tory delight. And the failure of a combined American-French assault on the British garrison, under the command of General Robert Pigot, at Newport, Rhode Island, produced a Loyalist barb that was popular on both sides of the Atlantic.

The expedition, in August of 1778, with 10,000 rebel troops under the command of General John Sullivan and a French fleet commanded by Count d'Estaing, was a disaster, although the British garrison numbered but 3,000. A combination of military ineptitude on the part of Sullivan, distinctly cautious behavior by the French commander, rivalry between the two, the unexpected intervention of a British fleet at the crucial point in the battle, and a 48-hour storm which severely punished the American troops all contributed to the fiasco.

A tendency by the Americans to blame the French commander for the defeat posed a serious threat to the recently concluded alliance between King Louis and the rebel forces. Whoever was to blame, it is clear that d'Estaing was not a distinguished sea fighter since all three expeditions against the British with which he was associated produced only negligible results.

The song appeared in Rivington's newspaper, October 3, 1778, and attempted to belittle the significance of the entire French Alliance, although it was clear that support from France offered the colonists their greatest hope for success.

Yankee Doodle's Expedition to Rhode Island [15]

Tune: "Yankee Doodle"

From Louis, Monsieur Gerard [16] came,
To Congress in this town, sir,
They bowed to him, and he to them,
And then they all sat down, sir.
"Begar," said Monsieur, "one *grand coup*
You shall *bientot* behold, sir,"
This was believed as gospel true,
And Jonathan felt bold, sir.

So Yankee Doodle did forget
The sound of British drum, sir,
How oft it made him quake and sweat
In spite of Yankee rum, sir.
He took his wallet on his back,
His rifle on his shoulder,
And vowed Rhode Island to attack
Before he was much older.

In dread array, their tattered crew
Advanced with colors spread, sir,
Their fifes played Yankee-doodle-doo,
King Hancock at their head, sir.
What numbers bravely crossed the seas,
I cannot well determine,
A swarm of rebels and of fleas,
And every other vermin.

Their mighty hearts might shrink, they thought,
For all flesh only grass is,
A piteous store they therefore brought
Of whiskey and molasses.
They swore they'd make bold Pigot squeak,
So did their good ally, sir,
And take him pris'ner in a week,
But that was all my eye, sir.

As Jonathan so much desired
To shine in martial story,
D'Estaing with *politesse* retired,
To leave him all the glory.
He left him what was better yet,
At least it was more use, sir,
He left him for a quick retreat,
A very good excuse, sir.

To stay unless he ruled the sea,
He thought would not be right, sir,
And Continental troops said he,
On islands should not fight, sir.
Another cause with these combined,
To throw him in the dumps, sir,
For Clinton's name alarmed his mind
And made him stir his stumps, sir.

There were undoubtedly many whose principles and loyalties changed with the fortunes of war. Careerists and opportunists abound during a time of rebellion when it seems as though first the insurrectionaries will win and then that the forces of the existing order will prevail.

In such circumstances, it would have been odd if some colonial tunesmith did not make a timely adaptation of one of the most popular songs in the English-speaking world of the time, "The Vicar of Bray." No one has ever been able to satisfactorily identify the original subject of this song—if, indeed, a particular person was its intended model. Although written early in the eighteenth century, supposedly during the reign of George I, the original ballad recounts the shifts in religious affiliation from Catholicism to Protestantism and back again several times over as the varying climates of religious sway shifted during the reigns of Charles I and Charles II, William and Mary, Anne and George I. Some suggest that the theme goes back to the days of Henry VIII.

In any event, its adaptation to the shifting loyalties of Colonial America during the Revolution was duly commemorated in an issue of Rivington's *Royal Gazette* for June 30, 1779.

The American Vicar of Bray [17]

When Roy - al— George ruled o'er this land, And— loy - al - ty no harm meant, For
Church and— King I made a stand and— so I got pre - fer - ment. I
still op - posed all par - ty—tricks, For rea - sons— I thought—clear ones, And
swore it— was their pol - i - tics To— make us Pres - by - tar - ians, And

Chorus:

this is law, that I'll main - tain, Un - til my— dy - ing— day, sir, Let
what-so - ev - er king may reign, Still I'll be the Vi-car of Bray, sir!

When Stamp Act passed the Parliament
To bring some grist to mill, sir,
To back it was my firm intent,
But soon there came repeal, sir.
I quickly joined the common cry
That we should all be slaves, sir,
The House of Commons was a sty,
The King and Lords were knaves, sir.

Now all went smooth, as smooth could be,
I strutted and looked big, sir,
And when they laid a tax on tea,
I was believed a Whig, sir.
I laughed at all the vain pretense
Of taxing at this distance,
And swore before I'd pay my pence,
I'd make a firm resistance. *(Cho.)*

A Congress now was quickly called
That we might act together,
I thought that Britain would, appalled,
Be glad to make fair weather.
And soon repeal th' obnoxious bill
As she had done before, sir,
That we might gather wealth at will,
And so be taxed no more, sir. *(Cho.)*

But Britain was not quickly scared,
She told another story,
When Independence was declared,
I figured as a Tory;
Declared it was rebellion base
To take up arms—I cursed it,
For, faith, it seemed a settled case
That we should soon be worsted. *(Cho.)*

When penal laws were passed by vote,
I thought the test a grievance,
Yet sooner than I'd lose a groat,
I swore the state allegiance.
The thin disguise could hardly pass,
For I was much suspected,
I felt myself much like the ass
In lion's skin detected. *(Cho.)*

The French Alliance now came forth,
The papists flocked in shoals, sir,
Friseures, Marquis, Valets of Birth,
And priests to save our souls, sir.
Our "good ally" with tow'ring wing
Embraced the flatt'ring hope, sir,
That we should own him for our King,
And then invite the Pope, sir. *(Cho.)*

When Howe with drum and great parade
Marched through this famous town, sir,
I cried, "May fame his temples shade
With laurels for a crown, sir."
With zeal I swore to make amends
To good old constitution,
And drank confusion to the friends
Of our late Revolution. *(Cho.)*

But poor Burgoyne announced my fate,
The Whigs began to glory,
I now bewailed my wretched state
That e'er I was a Tory.
By night the British left the shore
Nor cared for friends a fig, sir,
I turned the cat in pan once more,
And so became a Whig, sir. *(Cho.)*

I called the army butch'ring dogs,
A bloody tyrant King, sir,
The Commons, Lords, a set of rogues
That all deserved to swing, sir.
Since fate has made us great and free,
And Providence can't falter,
So Cong. till death my king shall be,
Unless the times shall alter. *(Cho.)*

chapter VI

The Folks On T'Other Side of The Wave

The Songs They Sang in England

To many in England, the crown's attempt to suppress the American rebellion was a cause of deep anguish. Many considered the Yankee cause to be just and sympathized with the striving for independence and civil liberty. Even more found the cost of the war— in lives lost, homes disrupted, monies spent—incompatible with the real interests of Britain. In addition, the war in America pitted Englishman against Englishman, giving rise to a sense of indentification with the American citizenry.

George III was himself an anachronism, a pale shadow of powerful royalty in an age during which royal power was sharply curbed. His Tory ministers were, for the most part, small-minded men with little understanding of the historical processes whose unwitting instruments they proved to be.

Criticism of the war and the government was widespread. The Whig opposition saw that a policy of unreason was going to cost

England her prized North American possessions—and yet they were helpless in the face of a determined Tory administration that continually underestimated the scope and depth of the rebellion until it was too late. Satires, poems, songs and broadsides critical of the war flourished in England during this period. Undoubtedly, many a Whig politician turned to rhymes when efforts in the Parliament proved futile. And as the news came back of growing rebel resistance, of battles lost, of the ineffectiveness of British generals, the street poets and singers likewise chimed in.

One political rhymester addressed himself to Parliament with the following song, signed only "M" in the *Middlesex Journal,* in 1776. He prefaced his song by saying, "Heaven help us if they will not take good advice, or stop for reflection, for they are speedily leading us to the devil."

To the Commons [1]

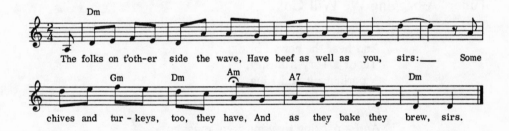

The folks on t'oth-er side the wave, Have beef as well as you, sirs:— Some chives and tur-keys, too, they have, And as they bake they brew, sirs.

What though your cannon raze their towns
And tumble down their houses,
They'll fight like devils, blood and bones,
For children and for spouses.

Another truth—nay, 'tis no boast,
Nor yet the lie o' the day, sirs,
The saints on Massachusetts coast
Gain if they run away, sirs. [2]

For further than your bullets fly,
A common man may run, sirs,
And wheat will grow beneath the sky
Where cannot reach a gun, sirs.

Then what are ships and swords and guns,
And men of bloody mind, sirs,
While, Parthian-like, who conquers runs,
Who loses—stays behind, sirs.

Recall your ships, your troops recall,
Let friends each other nourish,
So shall old England rule the ball
And George and freedom flourish.

"To the Commons" was fairly circumspect in its attacks on the Tories, and the author had the good caution to close with a statement of loyalty to the crown. But not so the anonymous shopkeeper who penned the following song. High treason runs through almost every stanza of the broadside ballad.

A Dose for the Tories[3]

Tune: "A-begging We Will Go"

Come hither, brother tradesmen,
And hear the news I bring;
'Tis of a Tory Ministry,
A parliament and King.

Chorus:
And a-packing they must go, must go,
Or a-begging we shall go.

With places and with pensions,
Like Charles and James of old;
They rob us of our liberties
And sell us all for gold. *(Cho.)*

The Jacobites and Tories,
Dance round us hand in hand,
Like locusts, they surround the throne,
And fatten on the land. *(Cho.)*

Our brothers in America,
With tyranny they grieve;
And then to make us praise their deeds,
With lies they us deceive. *(Cho.)*

Their ports and harbors they've blocked up,
And all their trade they stop,
So all the poor are left to starve,
And we must shut up shop. *(Cho.)*

With popery and slavery,
America they treat,
And swear they will dragoon them all,
If they will not submit. *(Cho.)*

Our soldiers and our sailors,
Their purpose will not suit,
They'll ne'er against the people fight,
For Mansfield[4] or for Bute.[5] *(Cho.)*

Our merchants have petitioned,
And all the towns beside;
And Chatham[6] has upbraided them,
But nothing bends their pride. *(Cho.)*

Then let us to the Palace
And Parliament repair,
And see who will deny us right,
Or tell us if they dare:

That a-begging we may go,
A-begging we may go,
A-begging we may go, go, go,
That a-begging we may go.

Should they our just request refuse,
Genius of liberty,
Conduct such traitors to the block,
A sacrifice to thee.

Then a-singing we will go,
A-singing we will go,
A-singing we will go, go, go,
And a-singing we will go.

That war profiteering played no small part in the determination of some to pursue the conflict is the suggestion of another song, "The Trading War."

To get a snug penny, since fighting began,
The war to encourage seems far the best plan;
For war is a trade, I'll uphold it, by which,
Though thousands grow poor, many hundreds get rich.

In fact, says the anonymous bard, many of the businessmen had no interest in seeing the war end and were concerned lest the British generals prove overzealous in their tasks:

If rumor says true, all the fear that was shewn,
Was that of their doing the business too soon.

Another broadside, nominally written by a British seaman, indicates that refusal to fight in a colonial war is hardly a recent development.

The Sailor's Address[7]
Tune: "Hearts of Oak"

Come listen, my cocks, to a brother and friend,
One and all to my song, gallant sailors attend;
Sons of freedom ourselves, let's be just as we're brave,
Nor America's freedom attempt to enslave.

Chorus:
Firm as oak are our hearts,
When true glory depends,
Steady, boys, steady,
We will always be ready,
To fight all our foes,
Not to murder our friends.

True glory can ne'er in this quarrel be won,
If New England we conquer, Old England's undone;
On our brethren, then why attempt to fix chains,
For the blood of Great Britain flows warm in their veins. *(Cho.)*

Shall courtiers' fine speeches prevail to divide
Our affections from those who have fought by our side;
And who often have joined us to sink in the Main
The proud boasting navies of France and of Spain. *(Cho.)*

Near relations of some who at court now do thrive,
The Pretender did join in the year 'forty-five;
And many in favor, disguised by high names,
Though they roar out for George, in their hearts are for James. *(Cho.)*

Of such men as these, let us scorn to be tools,
Dirty work to perform—do they take us for fools?
Brave sailors are wiser than thus to be bambed,
Let 'em turn out themselves, lads, and fight and be damned! *(Cho.)*

To the ground may disputes with our Colonies fall,
And George long in splendor, reign King of us all;
And may those who would set the two lands by the ears,
Be put in the bilboes and brought to the jeers. *(Cho.)*

A somewhat gentler barb—although not without its sting—was this piece which is reported to have been widely circulated both in England and America.

The Heads [8]
Tune: "Derry Down"

Ye wrong heads and strong heads, attend to my strains,
Ye clear heads and queer heads, and heads without brains;
Ye thick skulls and quick skulls, and heads great and small,
And ye heads that aspire to be heads over all.
    Derry down, down, hey derry down!

Ye ladies—I would not offend for the world,
Whose bright heads and light heads are feathered and curled,
The mighty dimensions dame Nature surprise,
To find she'd so grossly mistaken the size.

Enough might be said, durst I venture my rhymes,
On crowned heads and round heads of these modern times;
This slippery path let me cautiously tread—
The neck else may answer, perhaps, for the head.

The heads of the church and the heads of the state
Have taught much and wrought much—too much to repeat;
On the neck of corruption uplifted, 'tis said,
Some rulers, alas! are too high by the head.

Ye schemers and dreamers of politic things,
Projecting the downfall of kingdoms and kings—
Can your wisdom declare how this body is fed,
When the members rebel and wage war with the head?

Expounders, confounders, and heads of the law,
I bring case in point, do not point out a flaw;
If reason is treason, what plea shall I plead?
To your chief I appeal—for your chief has a head.

On Britannia's bosom sweet Liberty smiled,
The parent grew strong while she fostered the child,
Neglecting her offspring, a fever she bred,
Which contracted her limbs and distracted her head.

Ye learned state doctors, your labors are vain,
Proceeding by bleeding to settle her brain;
Much less can your art the lost members restore,
Amputation must follow—perhaps something more.

Pale Goddess of Whim! When with cheeks lean or full,
Thy influence seizes an Englishman's skull,
He blunders, yet wonders his schemes ever fail,
Though often mistaking the head for the tail.
    Derry down, down, hey derry down!

While George III and his Tory ministers represented traditional British imperial rule, their Whig counterparts favored a strategy of neocolonialism. Understanding that America could not be ruled by London effectively, they opposed the repressive taxation and other measures pressed by the crown against the Colonies. By granting greater home rule and more of a voice to the Colonies, the Whigs believed that Britain's hegemony in North America would remain secure.

The difference between Whigs and Tories was not solely over the North American question, however. They represented two distinct trends within the British ruling class which clashed frequently on many political questions. In general, the Whigs favored increasing the power of Parliament and reducing the power of the crown; and in this sense, they encompassed the needs of the developing English bourgeoisie as opposed to the interests of the landed aristocracy.

Whig satirists seized on the events in the Colonies to ridicule the ineptitude of the government. Every British military setback in America was turned into a sally against the Tory government. The following was written in 1778 and published in the *London Evening Post*. It did not endear its annonymous author or the newspaper to Lord North or the king.

The Halcyon Days of Old England[9]

Tune: "Ye Medley of Mortals"

Give ear to my song, I'll not tell you a sto-ry, This is the bright er-a of old Eng-land's glo-ry; And though some may think us in pit-i-ful plight, I'll swear they're mis-tak-en, for mat-ters go right! Sing tan-ta-ra-ra-ra, wise all, wise all, ___ Sing tan-ta-ra-ra-ra, wise all, wise all. ___

Let us laugh at the cavils of weak, silly elves;
Our statesmen are wise men—they say so themselves.
And though little mortals may hear it with wonder,
'Tis consummate wisdom that causes each blunder! *(Cho.)*

They are now engaged in a glorious war,
It began about tea, about feathers and tar;
With spirit they push what they've planned with sense,
Forty millions they've spent—for a tax of three pence! *(Cho.)*

The debts of the nation do grieve them so sore,
To lighten our burden, they load us the more!
They aim at th' American's cash, my dear honey,
Yet beggar this kingdom and send them the money. *(Cho.)*

What honors we're gaining by taking their forts,
Destroying bateaux and blocking up ports!
Burgoyne would have worked 'em but for a mishap,
By Gates and one Arnold, he's caught in a trap! *(Cho.)*

But Howe was more cautious and prudent by far,
He sailed with his fleet up the great Delaware;
All summer he struggled and strove to undo 'em,
But the plague of it was, he could not get to them, *(Cho.)*

Oh! think us not cruel, because our allies
Are savagely scalping men, women and boys!
Maternal affection to this step doth move us,
The more they are scalped, the more they will love us! *(Cho.)*

Some folks are uneasy and make a great pother
For the loss of one army and half of another;
But, sirs, next campaign by ten thousands we'll slay 'em
If we can find soldiers—and money to pay 'em! *(Cho.)*

I've sung you a song, now I'll give you a prayer;
May peace soon succeed to this horrible war!
Again may we live with our brethren in concord,
And the authors of mischief all hang on a strong cord. *(Cho.)*

Another sarcastic ballad, undoubtedly of Whig origin, bemoaned Lord North's obstinacy in dealing with the rebels and gibed at the government's repeated claims of military success. They could discern light at the end of the tunnel of the North American rebellion.

The Etiquette [10]

Tune: "Springfield Mountain"

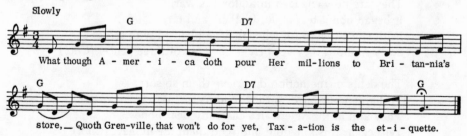

What though A-mer-i-ca doth pour Her mil-lions to Bri-tan-nia's store,— Quoth Gren-ville, that won't do for yet, Tax-a-tion is the et-i-quette.

The tea destroyed, the offer made
That all the loss should be repaid—
North asks not justice, nor the debt,
But he must have the etiquette.

He'd stop their port, annul their laws,
"Hear us," cried Franklin, "for our cause!"
To hear th' accused, the senate met,
Decreed 'twas not the etiquette.

At Bunker's Hill the cause was tried,
The earth with British blood was dyed;
Our army, though 'twas soundly beat,
We hear, bore off the etiquette.

The bond dissolved, the people rose,
Their rulers from themselves they chose;
Their Congress then at naught was set—
Its name was not the etiquette.

Though 'twere to stop the tide of blood,
Their titles must not be allowed,
(Not to the chiefs of armies met),
One Arnold was the etiquette.

The Yankees at Long Island found
That they were nearly run aground;
Howe let them 'scape when so beset—
He will explain the etiquette.

His aide-de-camps to Britain boast
Of battles—Yankee never lost;
But they are won in the Gazette [11] —
That saves the nation's etiquette.

Clinton his injured honor saw,
Swore he'd be tried by martial law,
And kick Germaine whene'er they met—
A ribbon saved that etiquette. [12]

Of Saratoga's dreadful plain—
An army ruined; why complain?
To pile their arms as they were let,
Sure they came off with etiquette!

Cries Burgoyne, "They may be relieved,
That army still may be retrieved,
To see the king if I be let;"
"No, sir, 'tis not the etiquette."

God save the king! and should he choose
His people's confidence to lose,
What matters it? they'll not forget
To serve him still—through etiquette.

There were some, of course, who celebrated the imperial cause. A loyal man of Kent employed the muse to sing old England's praises and ridicule Yankee pretensions. His lengthy ballad was published in the *Monthly Magazine* in London.

Ballad Of The American War [13]

Tune: "Chevy Chase" [14]

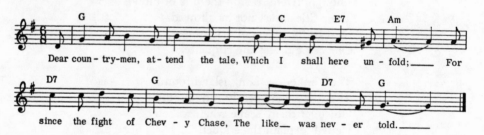

Dear coun-try-men, at-tend the tale, Which I shall here un - fold;_____ For since the fight of Chev - y Chase, The like_ was nev - er told._____

I know your loyal courage well,
All nations own the same;
Your precious lives you would not spare
To raise old England's fame.

Yet some there are beyond the seas,
Our fav'rite children late;
While they were true, we showed a love
No dangers could abate.

Our blood and treasure oft have flowed
To save them in distress;
Whene'er they called, then straight flew we,
Their inj'ries to redress.

But by their growing wealth and pow'r
How fatally misled,
"We'll set up for ourselves," cry they,
"And own no other head.

"If Britain, or her Parliament,
Disturb our mighty plan,
We'll make her rue th' unlucky day,
Prevent it how she can.

"We'll starve her manufactories,
And beggar all her poor;
For not a scrap of her vile ware
Shall touch our lordly shore.

"Tax us! O heavens! how dare she dream
Such grateful elves we'll be,
We'll make her tax herself to death
While we escape scot-free.

"She says, 'tis true, that we may raise
Our money as we please;
But not one farthing will we pay
Her tax-galled back to ease.

"We'll arm each Yankee in our realms
With trusty sword and gun;
And if she dare the cause dispute,
She'll surely be undone.

"Though she has long our mother been,
We'll soon her mistress be,
Destroy Old England's ancient power
And sink her in the sea."

"No, no, my friend, you vaunt too soon,
Old England scorns your boast;
She'll soon pull down your towering pride,
And rout your rabble host.

"We've still true blood in every vein,
As our forefathers were!
You've lately found it to your cost,
If you'll the truth declare."

Dear countrymen, I'll tell you how
This noble fight befell,
In which Old England's true born sons
Behaved themselves right well.

For by brave Wolfe's undaunted soul,
And his bold men, I swear,
'Twas hard to be controlled by those
Whose strength we sought to rear.

While Canada's waste and boundless wilds,
Ambitious France possessed,
The Yankees owned our sovereign rule,
And Britain's power caressed.

But when our arms, to save their lands,
Had driven the Frenchmen out,
They straight forgot our parent love,
And raised this horrid rout.

To quell their upstart sovereignty,
Our soldiers crossed the main;
For Boston harbor they were bound,
Which they did shortly gain.

The Yankees crowded every hill
At this alarming sight,
They looked and quaked, and for a while
Forgot their boasted might.

But when they saw our men so few,
Their dying hopes revived;
They swore they'd burn us in the town,
We should not be long-lived.

With this intent they straight repaired
To lofty Bunker's Hill,
Then came by night, and there intrenched
As mice demure and still.

From thence they hoped the town to fire
With their artillery,
But this brave scheme was soon destroyed,
As you shall shortly see.

Sly Gage, who saw their coward view,
Resolved to make them move;
He bade his merry-men fly to arms
And all their manhood prove.

Two thousand Britons, stout and bold,
Marched straight from Boston town;
Six thousand Yankees manned their lines,
Nor durst come further down.

Brave Howe and Clinton had the charge
Of this bold enterprise;
Lord Percy [15] scorns to stay behind,
Whether he lives or dies.

Old Putnam, [16] crafty as a fox,
And sullen as a bear,
The rebels formed, and thus he strove
To check their rising fear:

"Skulk close," cried he, "behind your lines,
And point your rifles well;
At yon bold Britons take your aim,
Leave none their loss to tell.

"If they can 'scape our levelled balls,
Or hit what they can't see,
Though better men ne'er took the field,
The devil must in them be.

"But at their captains most of all
Direct your deathful shot;
When these are slain, their men will fly,
Or perish all, God wot!

"Their British dames shall rue the day
That brought them trooping here;
And sons their fathers' fate lament
With many a trickling tear."

Hereat the Yankees strove to shout,
And grinned a ghastly smile,
To see themselves so well prepared
By Britain's coward guile.

They swore their hearts felt bold indeed,
And they would shew it soon;
Not one Briton would they spare
To see the coming noon.

Meanwhile the British infantry
In order stood arrayed,
With drums and fifes playing merrily,
And colors full displayed.

In th' open plain they all appeared,
Not one looked cold or shy;
For to a man they were resolved
To conquer or to die.

Bold Howe, therefore, straight bade them charge
The rebel yeomanry;
For why? he saw through every rank
His men as bold as he.

"Britons, advance, advance," cried he,
"To charge yon trait'rous rout;
Though trenched and lined up to their teeth,
We soon shall drive them out.

"Your duty and your honor call,
To you more dear than life;
I say no more—march on, my men,
Nor fear th' unequal strife."

They swift obeyed with heart and hand,
As good men, and as true,
As ever charged a bayonet
Or e'er a trigger drew.

When they came near the Yankee lines,
Some five score yards or so,
The rebels fired, and British blood
In streams began to flow.

Oh, Christ! my very heart does bleed,
While I the scene renew;
One thousand true-born British men
Their murd'ring rifles slew.

Twice fifty captains too there fell
In that bloodthirsty day,
Some sorely wounded, and the rest
Turned soon to ice-cold clay.

Pitcairn, [17] the brave, his son bore off,
In mortal agony;
And Abercombie's [18] vet'ran heart
That hour was doomed to die.

Full many a gentleman beside
Lay gasping on the plain;
Nor wife, nor child, nor parent dear,
Shall they behold again.

Ev'n Howe, the gallant and the good,
Had shared their hapless fall;
But when the rebel took his aim,
An angel glanced the ball.

He in the front rode manfully,
No danger him dismayed;
And though some minutes left alone,
He scorned to be afraid.

For all his troops at first recoiled,
To see such hellish play;
But by his generous words and deeds,
He soon restored the day.

"Advance," he cried, "my countrymen,
Nor let it e'er be said,
To George our sov'reign lord and king,
His British boys have fled."

With that they rallied hand in hand,
One thousand warriors true,
And to the ruffian rebel lines
With manly vengeance flew.

Through showers of leaden hail,
Regardless of their fate,
And to revenge their comrades fall,
O'erleapt the parapet.

Hereat the Yankees in amaze
Straight to the rearward ran,
And he who had the nimblest heels
Was thought the stoutest man.

With might and main they sped their way,
Nor cast one backward look;
Yet many hundreds in their flight
Our musquetry o'ertook.

The rest their hasty rout pursued,
Unto their second line,
Where deeply trenched, they halt perdue,
And all their forces join.

Thus nimbly 'scaped, loud victory
They shouted o'er the plain;
And when they were out of reach,
Their hearts felt bold again.

But if they're bold as they pretend,
Let them appoint the day;
We'll meet them in the open field,
And show them British play.

Though they come three to one, or more,
We will not flinch one jot;
But noble death, or vict'ry glad,
Shall be our happy lot.

Yet now forsooth, they boast aloud,
What mighty feats they'll do;
Forthwith they'll open all their ports,
To England's every foe.

Nor will they cease the rebel strife
On which their hearts are bent,
Until we pay the wilful cost
Of their proud armament.

But, by the Lord, ere this shall be,
We'll stretch our every vein,
And sooner spill our best heart-blood,
Than wear so foul a stain.

Oh! let Old England but support
Our loyal bravery;
We soon will end this horrid rout,
And make the Yankees fly.

Their dastard souls shall rue the day,
They brought us trooping here:
And their base folly they shall wail
With many a bitter tear.

For cursed be the heart and hand
Who fears the sword to take,
And use the same right manfully,
For brave old England's sake.

Old England, queen of all the isles,
And empress of the main,
Fair liberty's own darling child,
The scourge of France and Spain.

As long as river streams shall flow,
Or stars their courses run,
Old England's fame shall rise secure,
And fly from sun to sun.

Another pro-government ballad suffered from a certain astigmatism in its appraisal of the military capabilities of Britain's Yankee, French, and Spanish opponents. (On April 12, 1779 Spain declared war on England in an attempt to reclaim Gibraltar while the British were tied down in North America.)

A New Tory Ballad[19]

Tune: "Derry Down"

Rouse, Britons! at length,
And put forth your strength,
Perfidious France to resist;
Ten Frenchmen will fly
To shun a black eye,
If an Englishman doubles his fist.
Derry down, down, hey derry down.

But if they feel stout,
Why let them turn out,
With their maws stuffed with frogs, soups and jellies;
Brave Hardy's [20] sea thunder
Shall strike them with wonder,
And make the frogs leap in their bellies!
  Derry down, down, hey derry down.

For their Dons and their ships,
We care not three skips
Of a flea—and their threats turn into jest, O!
For we'll bang their bare ribs
For the infamous fibs,
Crammed into their fine manifesto. [21]

Our brethren so frantic
Across the Atlantic,
Who quit their old friends in a huff;
In spite of their airs
Are at their last prayers,
And of fighting have had quantum suff.

Then if powers at a distance
Should offer assistance,
Say boldly, "We want none, we thank ye,"
Old England's a match,
And more for old scratch,
A Frenchman, a Spaniard, a Yankee!

But despite these efforts, it was not a popular war. War profiteering, corruption and a cause which could not inspire Britons to fight all combined to create an atmosphere of discontent in England. A street broadside reflected the popular mood:

Come my sons, mourn with your mother
At the melancholy news,
From New York and other places
Where Britons now do rendezvous....

Nothing now but devastation
Is the prospect every way,
Kind heaven stop the desolation
In North Amerikay....

This is now the case of Briton,
Oh! gracious heaven stand our friend,
And in mercy shine upon us,
Bring these troubles to an end.

chapter VII

Revolutionary Postscripts

Songs of the New Nation
and the War of 1812

The shaping of the American nation in the wake of the Revolution's triumph was not an easy undertaking. With the erosion of the wartime unity between the states, much of the national spirit ebbed.

Clearly some form of union was desirable—in terms of military defense and commerce, at least. But the popular democratic sentiment unleashed by the Revolution and its rhetoric was suspicious of a strong federal government which would be removed from daily contact with the people. The people wanted power to reside with local and state government, where a careful eye could be kept on officeholders.

And so a sharp political struggle developed around the question of the constitution, with the Federalists urging a strong, centralized authority while others sought to curb the powers of the government then coming into being. But the interests of the merchants and manufacturers proved too strong for the farmers and artisans. The tide of history was with a developing capitalism that required a firmer central hand. Eventually, the Federalists won their strong constitution, but not before some important concessions—in particular, the Bill of Rights—had been won from them. In each state, constitutional conventions were called for the purpose of ratifying the document. Shortly after Massachusetts ratified on March 5, 1788, the following song appeared in local newspapers.

A Yankee Federal Song [1]

Tune: "Yankee Doodle"

> The 'vention did in Boston meet,
> But State House could not hold 'em,
> So then they went to Fed'ral Street,
> And there the truth was told 'em.
>
> *Chorus:*
> Yankee Doodle, keep it up!
> Yankee Doodle, dandy,
> Mind the music and the step,
> And with the girls be handy.
>
> They ev'ry morning went to prayer,
> And then began disputing,
> Till opposition silenced were,
> By arguments refuting. *(Cho.)*
>
> Then Squire Hancock like a man
> Who dearly loves the nation,
> By a concil'atory plan,
> Prevented much vexation. *(Cho.)*
>
> He made a woundy [2] Fed'ral speech,
> With sense and elocution;
> And then the 'vention did beseech
> T'adopt the Constitution. *(Cho.)*
>
> The question being outright put,
> (Each voter independent),
> The Fed'ralists agreed t'adopt,
> And then propose amendment. *(Cho.)*

The other party seeing then
The people were against 'em,
Agreed like honest, faithful men,
To mix in peace amongst 'em. (Cho.)

The Boston folks are deuced lads,
And always full of notions;
The boys, the girls, their mams and dads
Were filled with joy's commotions. (Cho.)

So straightway they procession made,
Lord! how nation fine, sir,
For every man of every trade
Went with his tools—to dine, sir. (Cho.)

Oh, then a whapping feast began,
And all hands went to eating;
They drank their toasts, shook hands, and sung,
Huzza! for 'vention meeting! (Cho.)

Now politicians of all kinds
Who are not yet decided,
May see how Yankees speak their minds
And yet are not divided. (Cho.)

Then from this sample let 'em cease
Inflammatory writing,
For freedom, happiness and peace
Is better far than fighting. (Cho.)

So here I end my Fed'ral song,
Composed of thirteen verses;
May agriculture flourish long,
And commerce fill our purses! (Cho.)

For a while the "inflammatory writing" did die down. Washington's accession to the presidency helped restore unity to the new nation. But the class and sectional conflicts were only momentarily muted. When John Adams succeeded Washington, the struggle emerged again, with Thomas Jefferson leading the opposition. But meanwhile, Americans were enjoying themselves with songs like this one.

The Hobbies[3]

Words and music: Williamson[4]

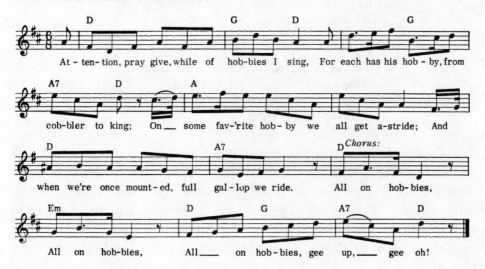

At-ten-tion, pray give, while of hob-bies I sing, For each has his hob-by, from cob-bler to king; On some fav-'rite hob-by we all get a-stride; And when we're once mount-ed, full gal-lop we ride. All on hob-bies,

Chorus: All on hob-bies, All on hob-bies, gee up, gee oh!

Some hobbies are restive and hard for to govern,
E'en just like our wives, they're so cursedly stubborn;
The hobbies of scolds are their husbands to tease,
And the hobbies of lawyers are plenty of fees.
    That's their hobby, etc.

The beaux, those sweet gentlemen's hobbies good lack,
Is to wear great large poultices tied round the neck;
And think in the ton and the tippy they're dressed,
If they've breeches that reach from the ankle to chest.
    That's their hobby, etc.

The hobbies of sailors, when safe moored in port,
Are their wives and their sweethearts to toy with and sport;
When our navy's completed, their hobby shall be,
To show the whole world that America's free.
    That's their hobby, etc.

The hobbies of soldiers, in time of great wars,
Are breaches and battles, with blood, wounds and scars;
But in peace, you'll observe, that quite different their trade is,
The hobbies of soldiers in peace, are the ladies.
    That's their hobby, etc.

183

The ladies, sweet creatures, yes, they now and then,
Get astride of their hobbies, e'en just like the men;
With smiles and with simpers beguile us with ease,
And we gallop, trot, amble e'en just as they please.
    That's their hobby, etc.

The American's hobby has long since been known,
No tyrant or king shall from them have a throne;
Their States are united and let it be said,
Their hobby is Washington, Peace and Free Trade.
    That's their hobby, etc.

George Washington, as the major figure of national unity, was the subject for scores of compositions. As is usually the case with overly flattering paeans of this sort, none have lasted beyond the immediacy of their time. Typical was a lengthy tribute, composed to the tune of "God Save the King," written by "a citizen of Virginia" on the occasion of Washington's birthday. Here is the first verse and chorus:

Hail, godlike Washington!
Fair freedom's chosen son,
    Born to command;
While this great globe shall roll,
Thy deeds from pole to pole,
Shall shake Columbia's soul
    With virtuous praise.

Millions unborn to save,
Freedom to worlds he gave,
    Liberty's Chief!
Terrific God of War,
Seated in Vict'ry's car,
Fame hails him from afar,
    Virginia's boast.

But the accession to the presidency of John Adams shattered the deceptive calm of Washington's terms. Washington wielded power with the judiciousness and authority of a man whose place in history was already secure. He saw himself as a unifier; perhaps he understood that he was holding back the conflicts of section and class almost by the force of his personality alone.

But John Adams took office with no such mandate. The simmering conflict between the mercantile interests of the North and the agrarian interests of the South boiled up into an intense rivalry between Adams and Jefferson. In the developing conflict between England and France, Adams saw the country's future more attuned to the interests of her former master, while Jefferson, inspired by the ideals and sweep of the French Revolution, advocated an expansion of popular participation in government. The rivalry between the two intensified with the enactment of the notorious Alien and Sedition Acts of 1798, which gave the president sweeping powers in contravention of individual liberties—powers that were used particularly against pro-Jefferson newspapers and political societies.

A strident tribute to Adams, set to the tune of "Anacreon in Heaven" (later to be used for "The Star-Spangled Banner"), was composed by Robert Treat Paine, Jr., a Federalist songwriter so opposed to the leveling ideas then current that he had his name legally changed from Thomas Paine since he considered the well-known pamphleteer to be an "infidel."

Here is one verse:

> Let our Patriots destroy Anarch's pestilent worm,
> Lest our liberty's growth should be checked by corrosion;
> Then let clouds thicken round us—we heed not the storm;
> Our realm fears no shock but the earth's own explosion;
>   Foes assail us in vain
>   Though their fleets bridge the main,
> For our altars and laws with our lives we'll maintain.

Jeffersonians meanwhile were singing:

> Men in power too oft betray
> Full of wild ambition,
> Their commands we must obey,
> Or they'll cry—"Sedition."
> Not a censure must be heard,
> *Well-born men* must be revered.
>
> Independence cost us dear,
> Life, blood, toil and treasure,
> Sighs and groans and many a tear,
> And troubles beyond measure;
> Let no faction e'er arise,
> That would steal the precious prize.

> If you peace and freedom love,
> Act with circumspection,
> Every foe to these remove,
> At your next election;
> Choose for chief, Columbia's son,
> The immortal Jefferson.

But all was not faction and polemic. There were many, concerned over the divisions, who strove to restore a spirit of unity. That such a unity always redounds to the benefit of those in power was surely known, but the effort likewise reflected a genuine yearning to resolve the strains of conflict. It was such a spirit that gave rise to one of our first and most lasting patriotic anthems, "Hail Columbia." The author of the lyrics for this hymn was Joseph Hopkinson, son of Francis Hopkinson, the signer of the Declaration of Independence and one of the best-known composers in the Colonial period (see "The Battle of the Kegs" and "A Toast").

The song was written in 1798, and many years later, its author wrote the following account of its origins:

It was written in the summer of 1798, when war with France was thought to be inevitable. Congress was then in session in this city [Philadelphia], deliberating upon that important subject, and acts of hostility had actually taken place. The contest between England and France was raging, and the people of the United States were divided into parties for the one side or the other; some thinking that policy and duty required us to espouse the cause of republican France, as she was called; others were for connecting ourselves with England, under the belief that she was the great preservative power of good principles and safe government.... The spirit of party has never risen higher, I think not so high, in our country, as it did at that time, upon that question. The theater was then open in our city. A young man belonging to it, whose talent was as a singer ... called on me on Saturday afternoon, his benefit being announced for the following Monday. His prospects were very disheartening; but he said that if he could get a patriotic song adapted to the tune of the "President's March," he did not doubt of a full house; that the poets of the theatrical corps had been trying to accomplish it, but had not succeeded. I told him I would try what I could do for him. He came the next afternoon; and the song, such as it is, was ready for him. The object of the author was to get up an *American spirit*, which should be independent of, and above the interests, passions and policy of both belligerents: and look and feel exclusively for our own honor and rights. No allusion is made to France or England, or the quarrel between them: or to the question, which was most at fault in their treatment of us. Of course, the song found favor with both parties, for both were Americans; at least neither could disavow the sentiments and feelings it inculcated. Such is the history of this song which has endured infinitely beyond the expectation of the author, as it is beyond any merit it can boast of, except that of being truly and exclusively patriotic in its sentiments and spirit.

The singer's name was Gilbert Fox, and according to reports, his introduction of the song created a sensation. Seven encores were demanded, and by the last time, the audience was standing and joining in with full-throated zeal.

Hail Columbia [5]

Words: Joseph Hopkinson
Tune: "The President's March" [6]

Immortal patriots! rise once more,
Defend your rights, defend your shore.
Let no rude foe with impious hand,
Let no rude foe with impious hand,
Invade the shrine where sacred lies,
Of toil and blood the well-earned prize.
    While offering peace sincere and just,
    In heaven we place a manly trust,
    That truth and justice will prevail,
    And every scheme of bondage fail. *(Cho.)*

Sound, sound the trump of fame,
Let Washington's great name,
Ring through the world with loud applause,
Ring through the world with loud applause.
Let every clime to freedom dear,
Listen with a joyful ear;
    With equal skill, with god-like power,
    He governs in the fearful hour
    Of horrid war, or guides with ease
    The happier times of honest peace. *(Cho.)*

Behold the Chief who now commands,
Once more to serve his country stands—
The rock on which the storm will beat,
But armed in virtue firm and true;
His hopes are fixed on heav'n and you.
    When hope was sinking in dismay,
    When gloom obscured Columbia's day,
    His steady mind from changes free,
    Resolved on death or liberty. *(Cho.)*

While the new American nation molded itself into an uneasy union, Britain watched and waited, never completely resigned to the loss of the North American colonies. To be sure, there were more important matters to attend to, such as the widespread European unrest engendered by the French Revolution and the rising power of France under Napoleon.

At the same time, the Americans were thinking expansion. The Louisiana Purchase in 1803 only whetted their appetites for more. They looked south to Florida. They looked westward to the Mexican lands. But most of all, they looked north to Canada.

The British saw in the enterprising North Americans potential rivals for hegemony over the seas. It was British naval power and the vast domain of the British merchant fleet that was a cornerstone of Britain's place in the world.

The smoldering hostility between Britain and her former colonies reached a peak during the Napoleonic wars. The British proclaimed that neutral ships would not be allowed to trade with France unless they stopped at British ports first. They also announced their right to "impress" supposed deserters from the British Navy from other ships while on the high seas. This led to a series of events in which both deserting British seamen and Yankee sailors were physically kidnapped from American ships by British men-of-war. At the same time, the British were encouraging Indian tribes in the northwest to attack American outposts and settlements, supplying them with arms and money.

As the war fever mounted in the United States, the following song became popular.

Gunpowder Tea [7]

Tune: "Molly (Jenny) Put the Kettle On"

They'll get it strong, they need not dread,
Sweetened well with sugar of lead;
Perhaps it may get in their head,
    And spoil their taste for tea. *(Cho.)*

But should they set a foot on shore,
Their cups we'd fill them o'er and o'er,
Such as John Bull drank here before—
    Nice Saratoga tea. *(Cho.)*

Then let them come as soon's they can,
They'll find us at our posts, each man,
Their hides we will completely tan,
    Before they get their tea. *(Cho.)*

On June 18, 1812, at the urging of President Madison, Congress declared war on Britain. The provocations were, to be sure, real enough; but the "war hawks" in Congress undoubtedly believed that with England tied down by Napoleon on the European continent, it was a good time for the United States to make its move.

While it might seem that the American advantage would be in the land war directed against Canada and that British naval superiority would dominate the sea war, during the first year, at least, the contrary pattern unfolded. A series of startling naval triumphs over the British commenced with the historic engagement on August 19, 1812, between the U.S.S. *Constitution* and the British frigate, *Guerrière*, the latter actually a prize of war from the French. In a heated 30-minute battle off the coast of Nova Scotia, the *Constitution*, commanded by Captain Isaac Hull, completely vanquished the British ship, commanded by Captain James R. Dacres.

The victory electrified the Americans, especially in New England. A flock of songs and broadside ballads to commemorate the event welled up in the excitement. The very best of these ballads was adapted from a song popular among sailors at the time, called "Brandy-O." The original was a comic ditty which went, in part:

A landlady of France,
She loved an officer, 'tis said,
And this officer he dearly loved her brandy, O!
Sighed she, "I love this officer,
Although his nose is red,
And his legs are what his regiment call bandy, O!"

But when the bandy officer
Was ordered to the coast,
How she tore her lovely locks that looked so sandy, O!
"Adieu, my soul," says she,
"If you write, pray pay the post,
But before we part, let's take a drop of brandy, O!"

She filled him out a bumper
Just before he left the town,
And another for herself, so neat and handy, O!
So they kept their spirits up
By their pouring spirits down,
For love is like the colic, cured by brandy, O!

It was a good song for a celebration, and the unknown Yankee songsmith who changed it around created a ballad that became a favorite for decades among the sailors in the American merchant fleet.

The Constitution And The Guerriere [8]

Tune: "Landlady of France"

It oft-times has been told That Brit-ish sea-men bold
Could flog the tars of France so neat and han-dy-o!
But they nev-er found their match, Till the Yan-kees did them catch,
O, the Yan-kee boys for fight-ing are the dan-dy-o!

The Guerriere, a frigate bold,
On the foaming ocean rolled,
Commanded by proud Dacres, the grandee, O!
With as choice a British crew
As a rammer ever drew,
Could flog the Frenchmen two to one so handy, O!

When this frigate hove in view,
Says proud Dacres to his crew,
"Come, clear ship for action and be handy, O!
To the weather gage, boys, get her,"
And to make his men fight better,
Gave them to drink, gunpowder mixed with brandy, O!

Then Dacres loudly cries,
"Make this Yankee ship your prize,
You can in thirty minutes, neat and handy, O!
Twenty-five's enough I'm sure,
And if you'll do it in a score,
I'll treat you to a double share of brandy, O!"

The British shot flew hot,
Which the Yankees answered not,
Till they got within the distance they called handy, O!
"Now," says Hull unto his crew,
"Boys, let's see what we can do,
If we take this boasting Briton, we're the dandy," O!

The first broadside we poured
Carried her mainmast by the board,
Which made this lofty frigate look abandoned, O!
Then Dacres shook his head,
And to his officers, he said,
"Lord! I didn't think those Yankees were so handy, O!"

Our second told so well
That their fore and mizzen fell,
Which doused the royal ensign neat and handy, O!
"By George," says he, "we're done,"
And they fired a lee gun,
While the Yankees struck up Yankee Doodle Dandy, O!

Then Dacres came on board
To deliver up his sword,
Though loath was he to part with it, 'twas so handy, O!
"O! keep your sword," says Hull,
"For it only makes you dull,
Cheer up and let us have a little brandy, O!"

Now fill your glasses full,
And we'll drink to Captain Hull,
And so merrily we'll push about the brandy, O!
John Bull may toast his fill,
But let the world say what they will,
The Yankee boys for fighting are the dandy, O!

While Captain Isaac Hull was giving the Americans a victory to cheer about, another Yankee commander named Hull, General William Hull, was responsible for one of the most crushing military defeats in American history. Charged with organizing an invasion into Canada, Hull brought an army to Michigan in the summer of 1812. There he crossed the Detroit River and occupied the Canadian town of Sandwich.

In response, the Canadian governor, Sir Isaac Brock, organized an army of militia and secured the British alliance with the Shawnee Indians led by the great chief Tecumseh. The Indians forced Hull to retreat back to Detroit and then joined up with the Canadian militia for an attack on the Americans. The American army outnumbered the combined Canadian-Indian force by more than two to one, but the cagey Brock tricked Hull into believing that he had British regulars and an Indian army of 5,000 at his command. After the firing of but a few shots into Fort Detroit, Hull acceded to Brock's demand that the Americans surrender; and on August 15, 1812, the entire garrison of 2,500 men, with guns and ammunition, was turned over to the Canadian-Indian force, virtually without a fight.

Eventually Hull was court-martialed on charges of treason and cowardice and was convicted on the latter count. He was sentenced to be shot but President Madison finally spared his life.

An English parody to "Yankee Doodle" ridiculed the event this way:

Brother Ephraim sold his cow
And bought him a commission;
And now he's gone to Canada
To fi-ight for the nation.

Brother Ephraim, he's come back,
Proved an arrant coward,
Afraid to fight the enemy,
Afeared he'd be devoured.

But the lasting celebration of the American defeat was composed by a Canadian militiaman, described in one historical account as a Private Flumerfilt. The song became a favorite in the Canadian lumber camps where folk song collectors came across versions of it more than 100 years after the event.

Come All You Bold Canadians [9]

1. Come __ all you bold Ca-na-di-ans, I'd have you lend an ear, Con-cern-ing a fine dit-ty __ that would make your cour-age cheer, Con-cern-ing an en-gage-ment that we had at Sand-wich town; The cour-age of those Yan-kee boys so late-ly we pulled down.

There was a bold commander, brave General Brock by name,
Took shipping at Niagara and down to York he came;
He says, "My gallant heroes, if you'll come along with me,
We'll fight those proud Yankees in the west of Canaday!"

'Twas thus that we replied, "Along with you we'll go,
Our knapsacks we will shoulder without any more ado.
Our knapsacks we will shoulder and forward we will steer;
We'll fight those proud Yankees without either dread or fear."

We travelled all that night and a part of the next day,
With a determination to show them British play;
We travelled all that night and a part of the next day,
With a determination to conquer or to die.

Our commander sent a flag to them and unto them did say:
"Deliver up your garrison or we'll fire on you this day!"
But they would not surrender, and chose to stand their ground,
We opened up our great guns and gave them fire a round.

Their commander sent a flag to us, for quarter he did call,
"Oh, hold your guns, brave British boys, for fear you slay us all.
Our town you have at your command, our garrison likewise."
They brought their guns and grounded them right down before our eyes.

And now we are all home again, each man is safe and sound,
May the memory of this conquest all through the Province sound!
Success unto our volunteers who did their rights maintain,
And to our bold commander, brave General Brock by name!

But if American arms proved ineffective on land during the first year of the war, the fledgling U.S. Navy was giving a superb account of itself. In a series of sea encounters off the Atlantic coast, American commanders were besting their British counterparts in one-to-one engagements. Eventually, however, the superior British fleet was able to blockade virtually the entire Atlantic seaboard with disastrous effects on the American economy.

The first naval battle lost by the U.S. Navy took place June 1, 1813, thirty miles off Boston harbor, when the U.S. frigate *Chesapeake* engaged the British frigate *Shannon*. Both ships were of relatively equal size with a similar complement of crew. But the poorly trained and relatively inexperienced Americans proved no match for the British, who killed or wounded all the American officers. Captain James Lawrence of the *Chesapeake* was mortally wounded in the engagement, at which time he gave his last command, which has since become a motto of the U.S. Navy, "Don't give up the ship!" The Americans did not surrender, but the British finally boarded the *Chesapeake* and took it off to Halifax. The entire battle took but 20 minutes.

The following is a contemporary British account of the engagement. An extra dimension was added to the British triumph by having the song parody "The Constitution and the Guerriere."

The Shannon And The Chesapeake[10]

Tune: "Landlady of France"

Now the Chesapeake so bold,
Out of Boston, we've been told,
Came to take the British frigate neat and handy, O!
All the people of the port,
They came out to see the sport,
And the bands were playing Yankee Doodle Dandy, O!

The British frigate's name,
Which for the purpose came
Of cooling Yankee courage neat and handy, O!
Was the Shannon—Captain Broke,
All her crew were hearts of oak,
And at fighting they're allowed to be the dandy, O!

Now before the fight begun,
The Yankees with much fun,
Said they'd take the British frigate neat and handy, O!
And after that they'd dine,
Treat their sweethearts all with wine,
And the band should play up Yankee Doodle Dandy, O!

We no sooner had begun
Than from their guns they run,
Though before they thought they worked 'em neat and handy, O!
Brave Broke, he waved his sword,
Crying, "Now, my lads, we'll board,
And we'll stop their playing Yankee Doodle Dandy, O!"

We no sooner heard the word
Than we all jumped aboard,
And tore down the colors neat and handy, O!
Notwithstanding all their brag
O'er the glorious British flag,
At the Yankee mizzen-peak it looked the dandy, O!

Here's a health to Captain Broke,
And all the hearts of oak
That took the Yankee frigate neat and handy, O!
And may we always prove
That in fighting and in love,
The true British sailor is the dandy, O!

The most important naval battle of the war was fought, not on the high seas, but in the waters of Lake Erie. There, on September 10, 1813, an American fleet commanded by Commodore Oliver Hazard Perry defeated a British squadron of six ships under the command of Captain Robert H. Barclay. The engagement proved crucial, not only to the American cause but to long-range American interests in the entire Great Lakes and Old Northwest areas. As a result of Perry's triumph, the British were forced to evacuate Detroit, thus canceling out the earlier American military reverses. Ultimately, it guaranteed that the United States would not be compelled to cede any territory to the British at the cessation of hostilities.

The battle itself has been recounted many times and has been celebrated in scores of ballads and songs. Perry's flagship, the *Lawrence*, was named for the fallen commander of the *Chesapeake*. At the end of the engagement, Perry sent his famous message to General William Henry Harrison: "We have met the enemy, and they are ours; two ships, two brigs, one schooner and one sloop."

Perry's Victory [11]

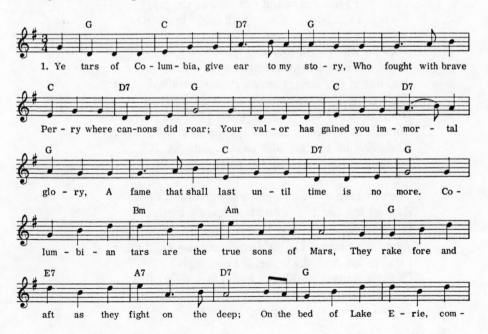

1. Ye tars of Co-lum-bia, give ear to my sto-ry, Who fought with brave Per-ry where can-nons did roar; Your val-or has gained you im-mor-tal glo-ry, A fame that shall last un-til time is no more. Co-lum-bi-an tars are the true sons of Mars, They rake fore and aft as they fight on the deep; On the bed of Lake E-rie, com-

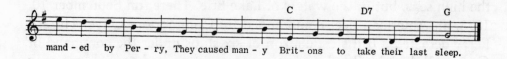

mand - ed   by   Per - ry,   They caused man - y   Brit - ons   to   take their last sleep.

'Twas just at sunrise, and a glorious day,
Our squadron at anchor, snug in Put-in-Bay;
When we saw the bold Britons and cleared for a bout,
Instead of Put-in, by the Lord, we put out.
Up went Union Jack, never up there before,
"Don't give up the ship!" was the motto it bore;
And as soon as that motto our gallant lads saw,
They thought of their Lawrence and shouted, "Huzza!"

O, then, 'twould have raised your hat three inches higher,
To see how we dashed in among them like fire;
The Lawrence went first, and the rest as they could,
And a long time the brunt of the battle she stood.
'Twas peppering work—fire, fury and smoke—
And groans, that from wounded lads spite of them broke;
The water grew red round our ship as she lay,
Though 'twas never before so till that bloody day.

They fell all around me, like spars in a gale,
The shot made a sieve of each rag of a sail;
And out of our crew, scarce a dozen remained,
But these gallant tars still the battle maintained.
'Twas then our Commander—God bless his young heart!—
Thought it best from his well-peppered ship to depart,
And bring up the rest who were tugging behind,
For why? They were sadly in want of a wind.

Then to Yarnall [12] he gave the command of the ship,
And set out like a lark on his desperate trip,
In a small open yawl, right through their whole fleet,
Who with many a broadside our cock-boat did greet.
I steered her and, damn me, if every inch
Of these timbers of mine at each crack didn't flinch;
But our tight little Commodore, cool and serene,
To still ne'er a muscle by any was seen.

Whole volleys of muskets were levelled at him,
But the devil a one ever grazed e'en a limb,
Though he stood up erect in the stern of the boat,
Till the crew pulled him down by the skirts of his coat.
At length, through Heaven's mercy, we reached the other ship,
And the wind springing up, we gave her the whip,
And ran down the line, boys, through thick and through thin,
And bothered their ears with a horrible din.

Then starboard and larboard, and this way and that,
We banged 'em and raked 'em and laid their masts flat;
Till one after t'other they hauled down their flag,
And an end put for that time to Johnny Bull's brag.
The Detroit and Queen Charlotte and Lady Prevost,
Not able to fight or run, gave up the ghost;
And not one of them all from our grapplings got free,
Though we'd just fifty-four guns and they'd sixty-three.

Now give us a bumper to Elliot [13] and those
Who came up in good time to belabor our foes;
To our fresh-water sailors we'll toss off one more,
And a dozen at least to our young Commodore.
And though Britons may talk of their ruling the ocean,
And that sort of thing—by the Lord, I've a notion—
I'll bet all I'm worth—who takes it? who takes?
Though they're lords of the seas, we'll be lords of the Lakes.

Among those who served with Perry during the historic battle was a young Marine by the name of James Bird. A volunteer from the town of Kingston, Pennsylvania, Bird, according to contemporary accounts, acquitted himself bravely and was wounded in the fight. Subsequently he was given a leave to go home.

After returning to service, he allegedly deserted a guard post while on duty. Captured and tried by court-martial, he was convicted, and along with two other deserters, executed aboard the ship *Niagara* in October of 1814. A considerable legend has grown up about Bird. Some claim that he overstayed his leave and that he was betrayed by a jealous rival in love. This last is a rather melodramatic account, however, and somewhat suspect. Others have suggested that the official War Department account of the case has been significantly weighted so as to justify his execution. President Madison refused to revoke the death sentence after reviewing the court-martial, apparently at the urging of military officers who were determined that a stringent example had to be made of Bird in order to check a lack of discipline in the ranks.

The text of the following song was the work of a Pennsylvania editor, Charles Miner, who printed it in his newspaper, *The Gleaner*, at Wilkes-Barre in 1814.

James Bird [14]

Words: Charles Miner

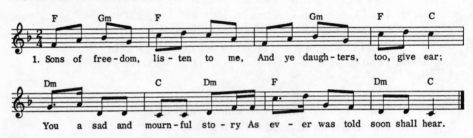

1. Sons of free-dom, lis-ten to me, And ye daugh-ters, too, give ear;
You a sad and mourn-ful sto-ry As ev-er was told soon shall hear.

Hull, you know, his troops surrendered,
And defenseless left the west,
Then our forces quick assembled
The invaders to resist.

Among the troops that marched to Erie
Were the Kingston volunteers,
Captain Thomas their commander,
To protect our west frontiers.

Tender were the scenes of parting,
Mothers wrung their hands and cried,
Maidens wept their swains in secret,
Fathers strove their hearts to hide.

But there's one among the number
Tall and graceful is his mien,
Firm his step, his look undaunted,
Scarce a nobler youth is seen.

One sweet kiss he snatched from Mary,
Craved his mother's prayer once more,
Pressed his father's hand, and left them
For Lake Erie's distant shore.

Soon they came where noble Perry
Had assembled all his fleet;
There the gallant Bird enlisted,
Hoping soon the foe to meet.

Where is Bird? The battle rages.
Is he in the strife or no?
Now the cannons roar tremendous,
Dare he meet the hostile foe?

Aye, behold him, there with Perry,
In the selfsame ship they fight;
Though his messmates fall around him,
Nothing can his soul affright.

But, behold! a ball has struck him,
See the crimson current flow,
"Leave the deck!" exclaims brave Perry,
"No," cries Bird, "I will not go!"

"Here on deck I took my station,
Ne'er will Bird his colors fly,
I'll stand by you, gallant captain,
Till we conquer or we die."

Still he fought, though faint and bleeding,
Till the stars and stripes arose,
Victory having crowned our efforts,
All triumphant o'er our foes.

And did Bird receive a pension?
Was he to his friends restored?
No, he never to his bosom
Clasped the maid his heart adored.

Soon there came most dismal tidings
From Lake Erie's distant shore.
Better, better had Bird perished
'Mid the battle's awful roar!

"Read this letter, dearest parents,
This will bring sad news to you;
Do not mourn your first beloved,
Though this brings my last adieu.

"Read this letter, brothers, sisters,
'Tis the last you'll hear from me.
I must suffer for deserting
From the brig *Niagar-ee.*"

Lo! he fought so brave at Erie,
Freely bled and nobly dared.
Let his courage plead for mercy,
Let his precious life be spared.

Dark and cloudy was the morning
Bird was ordered out to die;
Not a heart, not one felt sorry,
None for Bird would heave a sigh.

See him kneel upon his coffin,
Sure his death can do no good;
Spare him—hark! Oh, now they've shot him!
See his bosom stream with blood.

Farewell, Bird, farewell forever!
Home and friends he'll see no more.
Now his mangled corpse lies buried
On Lake Erie's distant shore.

The summer of 1814 turned out to be the grimmest period of the war for the American cause. With the defeat of Napoleon that spring, the British could turn their full attention to their former colonies. But in the early part of that year, especially after Perry's victory on Lake Erie, many thought that the British might be ready to sue for peace. It was then that the following song became popular. It was, presumably, written by an American seaman.

Ye Parliament of England [15]

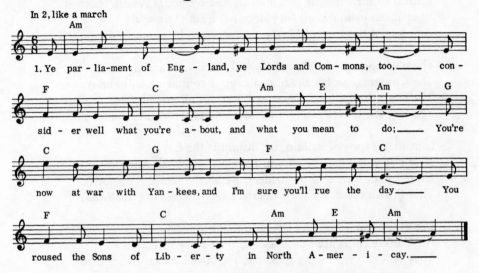

In 2, like a march

1. Ye par-lia-ment of Eng-land, ye Lords and Com-mons, too, _____ con-sid-er well what you're a-bout, and what you mean to do; _____ You're now at war with Yan-kees, and I'm sure you'll rue the day _____ You roused the Sons of Lib-er-ty in North A-mer-i-cay. _____

You first confined our commerce and said our ships shan't trade,
You next impressed our seamen and used them as your slaves;
You then insulted Rogers [16] while ploughing o'er the main,
And had we not declared war, you'd have done it o'er again.

You thought our frigates were but few and Yankees could not fight,
Until bold Hull the *Guerriere* took, and banished her from sight.
The *Wasp* then took your *Frolic*, you nothing said to that,
The *Poictiers* being off the coast, of course you took her back.

The next your *Macedonian*, no finer ship could swim,
Decatur [17] took her gilt-work off and then he took her in.
The *Java*, by a Yankee ship was sunk, you all must know,
The *Peacock* fine, in all her prime, by Lawrence down did go.

Then next you sent your *Boxer* to box us all about,
But we had an *Enterprising* [18] brig that beat your *Boxer* out;
We boxed her up to Portland and moored her off the town.
To show the sons of liberty this *Boxer* of renown.

Then next upon Lake Erie, brave Perry had some fun;
You own he beat your naval force and caused them for to run;
This was to you a sore defeat, the like ne'er known before,
Your British squadron beat complete, some took, some run ashore.

Then your brave Indian allies, you styled them that by name,
Until they turned their tomahawks, and by you, savages became.
Your mean insinuations they despised from their souls,
And joined the sons of liberty that scorn to be controlled.

There's Rogers in the *President*, will burn, sink and destroy;
The *Congress*, on the Brazil coast, your commerce will annoy;
The *Essex*, in the South Seas, will put out all your lights,
The flag she waves at her mast-head: "Free Trade and Sailor's Rights."

Lament, ye sons of Britain, far distant is the day,
That e'er you'll gain what you have lost in North Americay,
Go tell your king and parliament, by all the world it's known,
That British force, by sea and land's by Yankees overthrown.

Use every endeavor, and strive to make a peace,
For Yankee ships are building fast, their navy to increase;
They will enforce their commerce, the laws by heaven are made,
That Yankee ships, in time of peace, to any port may trade.

Grant us free trade and commerce and don't impress our men,
Give up all claims of Canada, then we'll be at peace again;
And then we will respect you and treat you as our friend,
Respect our flag and citizens, then all these wars will end.

But Britain had no intention of giving up Canada. Instead, the
coastal blockade was tightened even further and 14,000 battle-scarred
veterans of the Napoleonic wars were sent across the Atlantic to subdue
the Yankees. The British planned a three-pronged offensive: from the
north against Lake Champlain; along the coast, particularly centered
on Chesapeake Bay; and at New Orleans to throttle the Mississippi.
The coastal campaign had a great initial success with the capture and
burning of Washington on August 24th.

The British land invasion at Washington created panic all along
the Atlantic coast. In Philadelphia and New York, volunteer companies of militia sprang into being, and fortifications were hastily
constructed along the waterfront to guard against a British naval
assault. Samuel Woodworth, composer of the popular favorite, "The
Old Oaken Bucket," was living in New York and, inspired by the
"patriotic diggers" erecting the town's fortifications in Brooklyn,
composed the following song.

The Patriotic Diggers[19]

Words and music: Samuel Woodworth

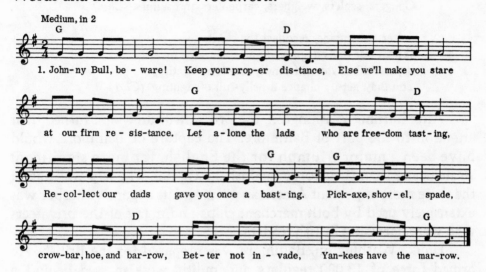

Medium, in 2

1. John-ny Bull, be - ware! Keep your prop-er dis-tance, Else we'll make you stare at our firm re - sis-tance. Let a-lone the lads who are free-dom tast-ing, Re - col-lect our dads gave you once a bast-ing. Pick-axe, shov-el, spade, crow-bar, hoe, and bar-row, Bet-ter not in - vade, Yan-kees have the mar-row.

To protect our rights, 'gainst your flints and triggers,
See on Brooklyn Heights, our patriotic diggers.
Men of every age, color, rank, profession,
Ardently engage, labor in succession. *(Cho.)*

Grandeur leaves her towers, poverty her hovel,
Here to join their powers with the hoe and shovel.
Here the merchant toils with the patriotic sawyer,
There the laborer smiles, near him sweats the lawyer. *(Cho.)*

Here the mason builds freedom's shrine of glory,
While the painter gilds the immortal story;
Blacksmiths catch the flame, grocers feel the spirit,
Printers share the fame and record their merit. *(Cho.)*

Scholars leave their schools with their patriotic teachers,
Farmers seize their tools, headed by their preachers;
How they break the soil—brewers, butchers, bakers,
Here the doctors toil, there the undertakers. *(Cho.)*

Bright Apollo's sons leave their pipe and tabor,
Mid the roar of guns, join the martial labor.
Round th'embattled plain in sweet concord rally,
And in freedom's strain, sing the foe's finale. *(Cho.)*

Plumbers, founders, dyers, tinmen, turners, shavers,
Sweepers, clerks and criers, jewelers, engravers,
Clothiers, drapers, players, cartmen, hatters, tailors,
Gaugers, sealers, weighers, carpenters and sailors. *(Cho.)*

Better not invade, recollect the spirit,
Which our dads displayed and their sons inherit;
If you still advance, friendly caution slighting,
You may get by chance a belly-full of fighting. *(Cho.)*

After burning Washington, the British withdrew and turned their attention to the port of Baltimore. The capture of Baltimore would have been a major triumph for the English, far more significant strategically than their foray against the capital. The city was one of the three most important American ports and its expansive harbor was extensively used by both merchant ships and many of the privateers who were harassing British traders.

Unlike Washington, Baltimore was prepared for the British. An armed force of 13,000 regulars and militia were massed behind a formidable system of defense works. Another thousand held Fort McHenry, where a line of sunken hulks kept the enemy fleet from the harbor. The British attacked by land on September 12, but suffered severe casualties while forcing the Americans to retreat. When the land forces withdrew, the British naval expedition undertook a massive naval bombardment of Fort McHenry on the night of September 13. This, too, was unsuccessful, and eventually the British withdrew from the Baltimore area, leaving Chesapeake Bay on October 14 for winter quarters in Jamaica.

It was the bombardment of Fort McHenry that inspired the writing of "The Star-Spangled Banner." The author, Francis Scott Key, was detained aboard a British ship at the time. He had gone there as a special emissary seeking the release of Dr. William Beanes, who had been taken prisoner by the British during the occupation of Washington. With preparations for the attack on Baltimore well under way, the British commander, General Robert Ross, decided to keep both Key and Beanes aboard. It was from the vantage point, therefore, of the deck of one of the ships in the British fleet, that Key watched "the bombs bursting in air" over Fort McHenry. Not until morning, when the American flag could be seen flying again over the fort, did Key know that the British attack had failed. Inspired by the moment, he wrote his famous poem which was subsequently adapted to the melody of an old British drinking song, "To Anacreon in Heaven." After being one of the most popular patriotic songs for more than a century, Key's song became the official national anthem of the United States in 1931.

The Star-Spangled Banner

Words: Francis Scott Key
Tune: "To Anacreon In Heaven"[20]

flag was still there. Oh! say, does that star span-gled ban-ner__ yet__ wave,__ O'er the land__ of the free and the home of the brave?

On the shore dimly seen through the mists of the deep,
Where the foe's haughty host in dread silence reposes,
What is that which the breeze, o'er the towering steep,
As it fitfully blows, half conceals, half discloses?
Now it catches the gleam of the morning's first beam,
In full glory reflected now shines on the stream.
'Tis the star-spangled banner, oh, long may it wave
O'er the land of the free and the home of the brave!

And where is that band who so vauntingly swore
That the havoc of war and the battle's confusion,
A home and a country shall leave us no more?
Their blood has washed out their foul footsteps' pollution.
No refuge could save the hireling and slave,
From the terror of death and the gloom of the grave.
And the star-spangled banner in triumph doth wave
O'er the land of the free and the home of the brave.

Oh, thus be it ever when freemen shall stand,
Between their loved homes and the war's desolation;
Blessed with vict'ry and peace, may the heaven-rescued land
Praise the power that has made and preserved us a nation.
Then conquer we must, for our cause it is just,
And this be our motto: "In God is our trust."
And the star-spangled banner in triumph shall wave
O'er the land of the free and the home of the brave.

The second prong of the British summer offensive was aimed
at northern New York State with Lake Champlain as its major objective. Control of the lake would have left the British with a major

toehold at the conclusion of hostilities. The British campaign, under the command of General Sir George Prevost, had an army of 11,000 plus a small fleet of 4 ships and 12 gunboats. The American force, under General Alexander Macomb, numbered but 3,300, while U.S. naval support was roughly the same as the British. The historic battle for Lake Champlain took place September 11, 1814 and was decided in a bloody naval encounter in which the U.S. fleet, commanded by Captain Thomas Macdonough, finally defeated the British. This left Prevost's superior force in an untenable position and the British were forced to retreat back to Canada, leaving behind great quantities of supplies. The British defeat at Champlain was decisive in bringing the war to an end on terms which added up to a stalemate; had the British won, they were prepared to insist on a peace treaty leaving them in possession of all territories they were occupying at the time.

A number of songs were inspired by the events. The best of these appeared in print as a broadside sheet, and while it was purportedly written from a British point of view, there is little doubt but that a Yankee composed it in consonance with an accepted practice of the time.

The Noble Lads of Canada [21]

Come all ye British heroes, I pray you lend your ears, Draw up your British forces, and then your volunteers; We're going to fight the Yankee boys by water and by land, And we never will return till we conquer sword in hand, We're the noble lads of Canada, come to arms, boys, come.

Oh, now the time has come, my boys, to cross the Yankee's line,
We remember they were rebels once and conquered John Burgoyne;
We'll subdue those haughty democrats and pull their
    dwellings down,
And we'll have the States inhabited with subjects to the crown.
    We're the noble lads of Canada, etc.

We've as choice a British army as ever crossed the seas,
We'll burn both town and city, and with smoke becloud the skies,
We'll subdue the old *Green Mountain Boys*, their Washington is gone,
And we'll play them "Yankee Doodle" as the Yankees did Burgoyne.
    We're the noble lads of Canada, etc.

Now we've reached the Plattsburg banks, my boys, and here we'll
    make a stand,
Until we take the Yankee fleet, McDonough doth command,
We've the *Growler* and the *Eagle* that from Smith we took away, [22]
And we'll have their noble fleet that lies anchored in the bay.
    We're the noble lads of Canada, etc.

Now we've reached the Plattsburg fort, my boys, and here we'll
    have some fun,
We soon shall take those Yankee lads, unless they start and run;
We'll spike all their artillery, or turn them on our side.
And then upon the Lake we triumphantly shall ride.
    We're the noble lads of Canada, etc.

Oh, our fleet has hove in view, my boys, the cannons loudly roar,
With death upon our cannon balls, we'll drench their decks with
    gore,
We've water craft sufficient to sink them in an hour,
But our orders are to board and the Yankees' flag to lower.
    We're the noble lads of Canada, etc.

Oh, what bitter groans and sighing we heard on board the fleet,
While McDonough's cocks are crowing, boys, I fear we shall get beat;
If we lose the cause by sea, my boys, we'll make a quick return,
For if they are true Yankee boys, we all shall be Burgoyned.
    We're the noble lads of Canada, stand at arms, boys, stand.

Now the battle's growing hot, my boys, I don't know how 'twill turn,
While McDonough's boats, on swivels hung, continually do burn;
We see such constant flashing that the smoke beclouds the day,
And our larger boats have struck, and our smaller run away.
    Oh, we've got too far from Canada, run for life, boys, run.

Oh, Prevost, he sighed aloud, and to his officers he said,
"I wish the devil and those Yankees could but sail alongside,
For the tars of France and England can't stand before them well,
For I think they'd flog the devil and send him back to dwell."
    Oh, we've got too far from Canada, run for life, boys, run.

Oh, Vermont is wide awake, and her boys are all alive,
They are as thick upon the Lake as bees around a hive;
For the devil and the Yankees, no doubt are all combined,
And unless we get to Canada, hard feed we shall find.
    Oh, we've got too far from Canada, etc.

Now prepare for your retreat, my boys, make all the speed you can,
The Yankees are surrounding us; we shall surely be Burgoyned;
Behind the hedges and the ditches, the trees and every stump,
You can see the sons of bitches, and the nimble Yankees jump.
    Oh, we've got too far from Canada, etc.

Now we've reached the Chazy heights, [23] my boys, we'll make a short
    delay,
For to rest our weary limbs and to feed our beasts on hay;
Soon McDonough's cocks began to crow, was heard at Starks' barn,
And a report throughout the camp was the general alarm.
    Oh, we're still too far from Canada, etc.

Oh, Prevost, then, he sighed aloud, and to his officers did say,
"The Yankee troops are hove in sight and hell will be to pay;
Shall we fight like men of courage, and do the best we can,
When we know they'll flog us two to one? I think we'd better run.
    Oh, we're still too far from Canada, etc.

"Now if ever I reach Quebec alive, I'll surely stay at home,
For McDonough's gained the victory, let the devil fight MacComb;
I had rather fight a thousand troops, good as e'er crossed the seas,
Than fifty of those Yankee boys behind the stumps and trees.
    Oh, we're still too far from Canada, etc.

"They told us that the Federalists were friendly to the crown,
They'd join our royal army and the Democrats pull down;
But they all unite together as a band of brothers joined,
They will fight for independence till they die upon the ground.
    Oh, we're still too far from Canada, etc.

211

"The old '76's have sallied forth, upon their crutches they do lean,
With their rifles leveled on us, with their specs they take good aim;
For there's no retreat in those, my boys, who'd rather die than run,
And we make no doubt but these are those that conquered John Burgoyne.
  When he got too far from Canada and had to run, boys, run.

"Now we've reached the British ground, my boys, we'll have a day
  of rest,
And I wish my soul that I could say 'twould be a day of mirth,
But I've left so many troops behind, it causes me to mourn,
And if ever I fight the Yankees more, I'll surely stay at home."
  Now we've got back to Canada, stay at home, boys, stay.

Here's a health to all the British troops, likewise to George
  Prevost,
And to our respective families and the girls that love us most,
To McDonough and Macomb and to every Yankee boy,
Now fill up your tumblers, for I never was so dry.
  For we've got back to Canada, stay at home, boys, stay.

The last major engagement of the War of 1812 was the Battle of New Orleans, which was fought January 8, 1815, some two weeks after the signing of the peace treaty between the Americans and the British at Ghent. But, of course, neither Andrew Jackson nor Sir Edward Pakenham, commander of the British forces, knew that.

Pakenham's assault on New Orleans was the third part of the British offensive strategy plotted out during the previous summer. It also proved to be the most disastrous. The British outnumbered the Americans, but the latter had the advantage of defending a site eminently suited to their own tactics, as well as the astute generalship of Jackson. In the final engagement, 5,300 British troops attacked 4,500 Americans effectively entrenched behind a line of hastily constructed breastworks. Jackson's sharpshooters from Kentucky and Tennessee greeted the massed British assaults with withering rifle-fire. In the half-hour battle, 2,036 British troops were killed or wounded, while American casualties totaled 8 killed and 13 wounded.

The battle rejuvenated American spirits, which had drooped considerably in the last months of the war, especially after the capture of Washington. It also made Jackson into a hero and eventually landed him in the White House. Many ballads of the battle were current, and one, "The Hunters of Kentucky," became Jackson's campaign song in the election of 1824. The one below was one of the best.

The Battle of New Orleans [24]

'Twas on the eighth of __ Jan - u - a - ry, Just at the dawn of day, We spied those Brit - ish __ of - fi - cers All __ dress'd in bat'l ar - ray; Old Jack - son then gave __ or - ders, "Each man to keep his post, And form a line from __ right to left, And __ let no time be lost."

With rockets and with bombshells, like comets we let fly;
Like lions they advanced us, the fate of war to try;
Large streams of fiery vengeance upon them we let pour,
While many a brave commander lay withering in his gore.

Thrice they marched up to the charge, and thrice they gave the
    ground;
We fought them full three hours, then bugle horns did sound.
Great heaps of human pyramids lay strewn before our eyes;
We blew the horns and rang the bells to drown their dying cries.

Come all you British noblemen and listen unto me;
Our Frontiersman has proved to you America is free.
But tell your royal master when you return back home,
That out of thirty thousand men, but few of you returned.

With the end of the war, the nation began an era of internal peace
and external expansion. And in its wake, a vast literature of songs
and poetry grew up, celebrating the exploits of those who fought
against the British in two wars. Once again the battles were fought;
once again the "embattled farmers" lived in words and music sung
by their grandchildren. If the heroes became even more heroic, if the
events became cloaked in even greater myth—such is the literature
of legend.

One elaborate ballad written immediately after the war, probably in 1816, provides a reasonably accurate recounting of the events of the 1812 War. Concededly, the song turned many lost battles into victories. And while it may be true that the United States didn't lose the War of 1812, neither did it win it.

Old England Forty Years Ago [25]

Words: Silas Ballou [26]
Tune: "The Girl I Left Behind Me"

Old England forty years ago when we were young and slender,
She aimed at us a mortal blow, but God was our defender;
Jehovah saw her horrid plan, great Washington He gave us,
His holiness inspired the man with skill and power to save us.

She sent her fleet and armies o'er to ravage, kill and plunder,
Our heroes met them on the shore and drove them back with thunder;
Our independence they confessed, and with their hands they signed it;
But on their hearts 'twas ne'er impressed, for there I ne'er could find it.

And since that time they have been still our liberties invading,
We bore it and forbore until forbearance was degrading;
Regardless of the sailor's right, impressed our native seamen,
Made them against their country fight, and thus enslaved our freemen.

Great Madison besought the foe, he mildly did implore them,
To let the suffering captives go, but they would not restore them.
Our commerce, too, they did invade, our ships they searched and seized,
Declaring also we should trade with none but whom they pleased.

Thus Madison in thunder spake, we've power and we must use it,
Our freedom surely lies at stake, and we must fight or lose it;
We'll make old England's children know we are the brave descendants
Of those who flogged their fathers so, and gained our Independence.

Our soldiers and our seamen, too, we've put in warlike motion,
Straight to the field our soldiers flew, our seamen to the ocean;
They met their foes on towering waves, with courage, skill and splendor,
They sunk them down to watery graves or forced them to surrender.

Decatur, Hull and Bainbridge[27] dear, did wonders in our navy,
Brave Captain Hull sunk the *Guerriere* and Bainbridge sunk the *Java;*
Decatur took a ship of fame high on the waving water,
The *Macedonian* was her name, and home in triumph brought her.

Perry with flag and sails unfurled met Barclay on Lake Erie,
At him, his matchless thunders hurled, till Barclay grew quite weary;
He gained the vict'ry and renown, he worked him up so neatly,
He brought old England's banners down and swept the lake completely.

Proud Downie[28] fell on Lake Champlain, by fortune quite forsaken,
He was by bold McDonough slain and all his fleet was taken;
Whene'er they met Columbia's sons on lakes or larger waters,
They sunk beneath her thundering guns, or humbly cried for quarter.

When Prevost saw he'd lost his fleet, he gave out special orders,
For his whole army to retreat and leave the Yankee borders;
Through dreary wilds, o'er bog and fen, the luckless gen'ral blundered,
He fled with fifteen thousand men from Macombs fifteen hundred.

Let William Hull be counted null, and let him not be naméd
Upon the rolls of valiant souls, of him we are ashaméd;
For his campaign was worse than vain, a coward and a traitor,
For paltry gold, his army sold to Brock, the speculator.

When Proctor found brave Harrison[29] had landed on his region,
Away the tim'rous creature run with all his savage legion;
But overtaken were, and most of them were killed and taken,
But Proctor soon forsook his post and fled to save his bacon.

At Washington their horrid crimes must tarnish British glory,
Children must blush in future times to read this shameful story;
They burned the volumes which comprised the best of information,[30]
Their barb'rous deeds will be despised by every Christian nation.

At Baltimore a deadly blow, the sons of mischief aimed,
The sons of freedom met their foe, and vict'ry justly claimed;
Amidst their ranks our thunder burst, many were killed and wounded,
Their chief commander bit the dust and all their schemes confounded.

What wonders did brave Jackson do when aided by kind heaven,
Their leader and four thousand slew, and lost but only seven;
Some interposing angel's hand repelled their vile intrusion,
The remnant of their broken band fled off in sad confusion.

They passed through numerous trying scenes, in most of them defeated,
Their grand defeat at New Orleans, the bloody scene completed;
Soon after this sweet peace arrived, our armies were disbanded,
Our scattered foes who had survived the war, were home commanded.

What has our infant country gained by fighting that old nation?
Our liberties we have maintained and raised our reputation;
We've gained the freedom of the seas, our seamen are released,
Our mariners trade where they please, impressments too have ceased.

Now in ourselves we can confide, abroad we are respected,
We've checked the rage of British pride, their haughtiness corrected;
First to the God of boundless power, be thanks and adoration,
Next Madison, the wondrous flower and jewel of our nation.

Next Congress does our thanks demand, to them our thanks we tender,
Our heroes next, by sea and land, to them our ranks we render;
Let us be just, in union live, then who will dare invade us?
If any should, our God will give His angels charge to aid us.

With the end of the War of 1812, American independence was secure. Indeed, one can hardly draw a line between the time the thirteen colonies fought for their independence and the time the process of continental and hemispheric expansion began. Nor need we try. The American Revolution, after all, brought to power a rising industrialist class whose vision of prosperity encompassed an entire world of markets and resources. The North American merchants, capitalists and landowners developed a philosophical outlook which went far beyond their immediate objective of a free enterprise economy.

From the beginning, the Revolution was built upon a profound contradiction. Fought for liberty, it reinforced the most odious system of chattel slavery known to the Western world. Fought for democracy, it replaced a class structure based upon aristocratic title and imperial appointment with one based on wealth and economic power. One points this out, not to diminish this revolutionary heritage, but to understand it in all its fullness. The illusion that the world's ideal state was brought into existence with the American Revolution deserves a discreet burial as the nation approaches its bicentennial. It was, after all, Thomas Jefferson who said:

God forbid we should ever be twenty years without such a rebellion.... The tree of liberty must be refreshed from time to time with the blood of patriots and tyrants.

216

Notes

Chapter 1

1. From the *Bay Psalm Book*, published in Boston in 1698, although the hymn is believed to have been current around 1674. The tune itself is more than a century older.

2. From a London broadside of the eighteenth century, but no exact date. (Library of Congress)

3. From a London broadside, ca. 1720. (Library of Congress)

4. This is a shortened version of an anonymous ballad written before 1720, possibly as early as 1690. The melody, which was used for other songs as well, is attributed to Samuel Ackroyde, a Restoration composer. From Thomas D'Urfey's *Pills to Purge Melancholy*, vol. 4.

5. A traditional New England ballad, first collected by Phillips Barry; see his *British Ballads from Maine*. Also known, in some versions, as "Billy Broke Locks."

6. From a broadside sheet of 1734 (New York Public Library).

7. The earliest reference to the tune is in Pepys's *Diary* under the date of January 2, 1664, where he mentions having bought "a ballet... made from the seamen at sea to

'The Ladies in Town'," unquestionably the same air. For an even fuller discussion of the circumstances surrounding this song and the next, see *Sing Out!*, vol. 5, no. 3.

8. Whiskey, from the Gaelic. The word may also have referred to a particular kind of Irish cordial.

9. Derogatory and, from the context, presumably sycophants.

10. The melody dates back to 1641, when a variant of it was used in the political warfare between the Puritans and the high church forces.

11. Folklorists Anne and Frank Warner learned this song from a New Hampshire woman, Mrs. Lena Bourne Fish, who told them, "This is an old song of the French and Indian War." The melody is from an Irish jig.

12. One of the oldest English-language folk songs indigenous to North America. This version is from an early broadside in the collection of the Massachusetts Historical Society. The original is believed to have been written shortly after the events.

Chapter 2

1. Although written originally in 1765 shortly after enactment of the Stamp Act, this song proved popular for several generations. The author himself added a dozen additional verses in 1779 in which he celebrated American military exploits. It was also popular again during the War of 1812.

2. Sir Frederick North (Lord North), lord of the treasury at this time, and subsequently chancellor of the exchequer and prime minister (1770-1782). He resigned after news of Cornwallis's surrender.

3. John Stuart Bute, British prime minister (1761-1763), and a particularly trusted confidant of George III. He came into the government with George's ascension to the throne in 1760. Even after retiring, Bute exercised considerable influence in the administration of his successor, George Grenville.

4. From Frank Moore, *Songs and Ballads of the American Revolution*, hereinafter referred to as Moore, *Songs and Ballads*. (See Bibliography.)

5. From Moore, *Songs and Ballads*. Slightly abridged. The original appeared in the *London Chronicle*, March 11, 1766.

6. From the *Boston Post-Boy & Advertiser*, April 14, 1766; also the *Virginia Gazette*, May of the same year.

7. From Frank Moore, *Illustrated Ballad History of the American Revolution, 1765-1783* (hereinafter referred to as Moore, *Illustrated Ballad History*), from which the two letters to Otis are also quoted. Moore's version of the song is taken from the *Boston Gazette* for July 18, 1768. The song also appears in the *Pennsylvania Chronicle*, issue of July 4-11, 1768.

8. From Moore, *Illustrated Ballad History*.

9. From Moore, *Illustrated Ballad History*. He reports that it was published in the *St. James Chronicle* in London, November 8, 1768, an interesting indication of the pro-American sentiment in England at the time.

10. From *The New England Psalm-Singer* (see Bibliography).

11. From Moore, *Songs and Ballads*. Reproduced, too, with the melody, in "Songs and Ballads of the American Revolution," by Lydia Newcomb, *New England Magazine*, vol. 13, no. 4, December 1895.

12. From the sheet music (New York Public Library), "as sung with unbounded applause by Mr. Andrews at the Federal Street Theater." Published by C. Bradlee.

13. From *Father Kemp's Old Folks' Concert Tunes* (see Bibliography), first published in 1860; but the song was already popular then and is considerably older.

14. Warren was one of the most prominent of the early revolutionary leaders, on a par with Samuel Adams and John Hancock. It was he who dispatched Paul Revere on his famous midnight ride. He became president of the Massachusetts Provincial Congress April 23, 1775 and head of the committee to organize an army.

15. From George Cary Eggleston, *American War Ballads and Lyrics* (hereinafter referred to as Eggleston, *American War Ballads*), vol. 1. (See Bibliography.)

16. From Moore, *Illustrated Ballad History*. The original "Rule Britannia" was composed by Thomas Arne in 1739 for the masque *Alfred*. The lyrics were by James Thomson.

17. From Moore, *Songs and Ballads*.

18. Tait was a judge in a minor court in Edinburgh when he wrote this song, supposedly on the departure of a friend for America. Years later, Robert Burns noted that "the song is well enough, but has some false imagery in it. ... In the first place, the nightingale sings in a low bush, but never from a tree; and in the second place, there never was a nightingale seen or heard on the Banks of the Dee, or on the banks of any other river in Scotland. Exotic rural imagery is always flat." Tait apparently took the criticism to heart, for in a later edition of the song, the second line reads: "And sweetly the wood-pigeon cooed from the tree."

19. From Moore, *Songs and Ballads*.

20. From Moore, *Songs and Ballads*. Moore made a composite from several broadsides published in 1775. The "Irishman" is undoubtedly a Yankee, although the anonymous author may well have been Irish.

21. The first two lines of the third stanza have been taken from the version in Frank Moore's *The Diary of the American Revolution*, ed. by John Anthony Scott (hereinafter referred to as Moore, *Diary*). (See Bibliography).

22. The "junto" was comprised of the three generals—Howe, Clinton and Burgoyne. The song appeared in the *New York Journal*, September 7, 1775. From Moore, *Diary*.

23. From Moore, *Songs and Ballads.*

24. This is a reference to the Newfoundland Fisheries Act of 1775, which closed those fisheries to New England seamen.

Chapter 3

1. For the best analysis of the obscure history of the song, see Oscar Sonneck's *Report on "The Star Spangled Banner," "Hail Columbia," "America," "Yankee Doodle,"* published in 1909, and the pamphlet by S. Foster Damon, *"Yankee Doodle,"* published in 1959. Damon's pamphlet has a reproduction of the Skillern broadside, from which the version here is taken.

2. From the complete text as quoted in Damon (see note 1 above).

3. From an early broadside titled "The Farmer and His Son's Return from a Visit to the Camp," reproduced in Damon (see note 1 above).

4. From Moore, *Songs and Ballads.*

5. A cheap, coarse-ribbed woolen material.

6. From Lauber, A. W., *Orderly Books of the Fourth N. Y. Regiment, 1778-1780,* as quoted in Thompson, Harold, *Body, Boots and Britches.*

7. An obsolete abbreviation for carriage or chariot.

8. The original has ten verses. These four have been excerpted from Moore, *Songs and Ballads.*

9. From Billings's *The Singing Masters' Assistant,* reprinted in many anthologies.

10. There were two British generals by the name, but Billings is undoubtedly referring to Richard Prescott, who was a particular object of American disdain.

11. First published in Dearborn's *Freeman's Journal* and reprinted in Moore, *Diary.*

12. There is no reference to a melody in the original, but the lyrics fit the pattern of many traditional songs. The tune here is adapted from a ballad popular among north woods lumberjacks.

13. Adapted and excerpted from a broadside sheet (New York Public Library). The original bears the inscription: "This was writ att Boundbruck March 13th A.D. 1777."

14. The original does not appear anywhere with a melody. If Franklin had a tune in mind, it must have been the most flexible of its period, since the verses are not consistent in their meter. Still, it vaguely fits the pattern of several melodies, such as "Villikins and His Dinah," which is reasonably close to that period. However, anyone interested in singing the song to this tune will have to make considerable

allowance for the irregular meter. To minimize this problem, the author has eliminated two or three verses from the original and made some slight adaptations in several other verses.

15. Prestonpans was the site of a historic rout of the royal army by Scottish rebels in 1745.

16. British General Hugh Percy, who participated in the battles of Lexington and Concord, where he led a relief column that helped protect the British retreat.

17. Lord Sandwich was first lord of the Admiralty during the American Revolution and earned a reputation for corruption and incapacity.

18. According to Moore, *Songs and Ballads*, from which this version is taken, the song appeared in papers of the period as "A New War Song by Sir Peter Parker." The melody here is taken from Moore, *Diary*.

19. The *Bristol*, Parker's flagship, was severely damaged in the encounter.

20. There are many sources extant for the ballad, including a number of broadsides, the works of Hopkinson, Moore's collections, etc. Moore, *Songs and Ballads* has considerable documentation of the particulars.

21. "Sir William" is General William Howe, who commanded the British Army that entered Philadelphia September 27, 1777.

22. Mrs. Loring was the wife of a Tory refugee from Boston, Joshua Loring, who as commissar of prisoners for the British earned an uneviable reputation for cruelty and harshness. In pseudo-discreet fashion, many early versions simply leave a blank space for the words, "Mrs. Loring," although it is clear that no one would have any difficulty in figuring out the reference.

23. Sir Erskine was British General William Erskine.

24. The original appeared in the *Pennsylvania Packet*, April 8, 1778. It has since been widely reprinted.

25. From Eggleston, *American War Ballads*, Vol. 1.

26. The word "indignity" is used here in its obsolete sense of "lack of dignity."

27. The text is from Moore, *Songs and Ballads*. Moore gives an interesting account of the entire Nathan Hale episode. The tune was adapted by Bill Bonyun and appears in Moore, *Diary*.

28. From Albert G. Emerick, *Songs for the People*. (See Bibliography.) Emerick reports as follows: "The words of this spirited song of the Revolution are taken from the Philadelphia *Saturday Courier*, from which we learn that it was written by an aide-de-camp of Mad Anthony. It was sung at the messes of the officers and soldiers; but the music to which it was sung is lost and forgotten. This loss we have endeavored to supply by an original composition, which we now [1852] offer to our patrons."

29. From the singing of John and Lucy Allison as recorded in *Ballads of the American Revolution and the War of 1812*, RCA-Victor. A very similar text appears in *The Soldier's Companion*, Leavitt & Allen, publishers, New York City, 1856.

30. Adapted from Moore, *Songs and Ballads*, whose text is credited to "a ballad sheet printed in 1783." The melody is provided in Moore, *Diary*, where it is described as a variant of "The Bonny Boy."

31. From Moore, *Songs and Ballads*, which has a detailed account of the entire episode.

32. Sir Henry Clinton, British commander in chief (1778-82), headquartered at the time in New York City.

33. From a nineteenth century broadside in the Harris Collection, Brown University, reprinted in Moore, *Diary*.

Chapter 4

1. From the singing of John and Lucy Allison, as recorded in *Ballads of the American Revolution and the War of 1812*, RCA-Victor.

2. From Downes/Siegmeister, *A Treasury of American Song*. (See Bibliography.)

3. From Moore, *Illustrated Ballad History*. Moore reports that "this song was written by a loyalist, yet it became a favorite with the provincials early in the war." He says that the words are to the melody of "The Muffled Bells of Bow and Bride," an air the author has not been able to locate.

4. From an anonymous broadside printed at Danvers, Massachusetts in 1776, reprinted in Moore, *Diary*.

5. Scott suggests that his tune for "The Battle of Trenton," an adaptation of the traditional ballad, "The Three Ravens," may be used for this song.

6. General Richard Prescott, captured by Montgomery's forces November 17, 1775.

7. Captain Jacob Cheeseman, an aide of Montgomery, who was killed at the same time.

8. General Guy Carleton, governor of Quebec, who is credited with having saved Canada for the crown.

9. From the singing of John and Lucy Allison as recorded in *Ballads of the American Revolution and the War of 1812*, RCA-Victor.

10. From Moore, *Diary*.

10a. General John Sullivan, whose military record included service in Boston and the unsuccessful invasion of Canada. He served with distinction in the Battle of Trenton.

11. Sir Guy Carleton.

12. John Murray, the fourth Earl of Dunmore, was royal governor of Virginia from 1770 until driven out by the rebels in 1776, at which time he returned to England.

13. One of the most popular ballads during the Revolution, many versions of this song have come down to us. This one is from Moore, *Songs and Ballads*. See also William L. Stone's *Ballads and Poems Relating to the Burgoyne Campaign* (hereinafter referred to as Stone, *Ballads*), p. 80.

14. Scott's version, similar to Stone's, is suggested as appropriate to the tune of "The British Grenadiers," but a number of others have adapted the song to the Irish "Brennan on the Moor," which is the melody provided here.

15. Major General Arthur St. Clair, who ordered the withdrawal of American troops from Fort Ticonderoga (July 2-5, 1777), an action much criticized at the time but subsequently vindicated by military analysts.

16. General Horatio Gates, the eventual victor in the Battle of Saratoga, subsequently involved in rivalry with George Washington.

17. General Nicholas Herkimer of the New York militia, fatally wounded in the Battle of Oriskany (August 6, 1777) during the Burgoyne campaign.

18. Really British Lieutenant Colonel Barry St. Leger, who commanded an expedition during the campaign.

19. Colonel John Brooks, who commanded a regiment of Massachusetts militia.

20. Benedict Arnold, whose role in this campaign was typically controversial.

21. Lieutenant Colonel Frederick Baume (his name is misspelled in the song), a Hessian officer under Burgoyne, who was sent to forage for supplies in Vermont, a raid that resulted in the Battle of Bennington, which ended in disaster for the Hessian troops.

22. Brigadier General John Stark, who led the American forces at the Battle of Bennington (see also "Riflemen of Bennington" with reference to "their leader Johnny Stark").

23. General Benjamin Lincoln, who played a key role in the Battle of Saratoga.

24. From Stone, *Ballads*.

25. The first two stanzas related to Burgoyne's colorful career before coming to America. The general was a military hero, a member of Parliament, a playwright and actor, a *bon vivant*, and widely respected by the British foot soldiers for his humanity in an age when British officers were better known for their harshness.

26. From George E. Hastings, *The Life and Works of Francis Hopkinson*. (See Bibliography.)

27. From S. B. Luce, *Naval Songs*. (See Bibliography.) Supposedly composed by a seaman at the time of the Revolution.

28. "The old Saltee's" is a reference to the Saltee Islands off the southeast coast of Ireland.

29. Text from Luce, *Naval Songs*. Melody from the singing of Frank Warner, who collected the ballad from C. K. Tillett of Wanchese, North Carolina, as it appears in Moore *Diary*.

30. From John Free, *The Political Songster* (1784).

31. In the eighteenth century interest charges of 10 percent on loans were considered usurious.

32. From Moore, *Songs and Ballads*.

33. The Marquis de Lafayette.

34. The reference to "red heels and long-laced skirts" may reflect the fact that some British officers had high heels and some British regiments wore kilts.

35. Admiral François Joseph Paul, Comte de Grasse, of the French Navy played an important role in the Battle of Yorktown.

36. Jean Baptiste Donatien de Vimeur, Comte de Rochambeau, was commander of French forces in North America during the Revolution and also played a role in the events leading up to the final battle.

37. From Moore, *Songs and Ballads*.

38. From *The Household Songbook* (1830).

39. Sir Henry Clinton.

Chapter 5

1. Information in general on the origins of the song is sketchy. Lewis Winstock in *Songs and Music of the Redcoats* (see Bibliography) reports a version in print as early as 1745, although he agrees that it must have been written at least 50 years earlier.

2. From *The American Musical Miscellany* (1798).

3. During the Napoleonic wars it was known as "Wolfe's Song" because of the legend. From two early sources: *The American Songster* (1788) and *The Baltimore Musical Miscellany or Columbian Songster* (1805).

4. From Winthrop Sargent, ed., *The Loyalist Poetry of The Revolution* (1857) (hereinafter referred to as Sargent, *Loyalist Poetry*).

5. The French governor of Canada whose surrender of Montreal September 8, 1760, concluded the French and Indian War.

6. William Shirley was Colonial governor of Massachusetts and for a brief period, commander of British forces in North America after the death of Braddock.

7. Apparently a regimental commander.

8. Robert Monckton, lieutenant governor of Nova Scotia in 1755 and Wolfe's second-in-command at Quebec.

9. British brigadier general.

10. From the singing of Mrs. Townsley, Bell County, Kentucky, 1917, recorded by Cecil Sharp and transcribed in *English Folk Songs from the Southern Appalachians*, vol. 2. (See Bibliography.)

11. Composite from a variety of sources.

12. From *Towne's Evening Post*, no. 435 (Philadelphia), as reported in Sargent, *Loyalist Poetry*.

13. From Moore, *Illustrated Ballad History*. No tune is given, but the song fits the pattern of many standard British melodies, including "Villikins and His Dinah."

14. From Moore, *Songs and Ballads*. The music is from *The Universal Magazine* for February 1771, as reported by Winstock, *Songs and Music of the Redcoats*.

15. From Moore, *Songs and Ballads*. Some sources ascribe authorship to John André.

16. Conrad Alexandre Gérard was the first French ambassador to the United States; indeed, he was the first representative of any foreign country to establish relations with the new nation.

17. From Sargent, *Loyalist Poetry*.

Chapter 6

1. From Moore, *Songs and Ballads*. The melody is furnished by Moore, *Diary*.

2. The third, fourth and fifth verses are particularly interesting because of their awareness of the strength of a national independence movement employing guerrilla-style warfare. The "saints on Massachusetts coast" clearly has Bunker Hill in mind.

3. From an anonymously published broadside (New York Public Library).

4. The Earl of Mansfield, a member of the British cabinet.

5. See Note 3, Chapter 2.

6. William Pitt, Earl of Chatham.

7. From a broadside sheet, printed in London (28 Great Tower St.), and also in Moore, *Illustrated Ballad History*. Moore cites a publication in the *Middlesex Journal* and also reports that an American ballad sheet containing the words and music was personally engraved by Paul Revere.

8. From Moore, *Songs and Ballads*.

9. From Moore, *Songs and Ballads*. The melody is from Claude M. Simpson, *The British Broadside Ballad and Its Music*. (See Bibliography.)

10. From Moore, *Songs and Ballads*.

11. The "Gazette" referred to is presumably Rivington's *Royal Gazette*, the leading Tory paper in the Colonies.

12. The antagonism between General Henry Clinton, one of the foremost British commanders in the field, and Lord Germain, British secretary of state for the American colonies, arose when the latter failed to defend Clinton from charges lodged by Admiral Sir Peter Parker that the general had failed to support his naval attack on Charleston. According to some historians, Germain was so anxious to avoid a quarrel or duel with Clinton that he arranged to secure the Order of the Bath for the latter, even though the order was full and he had to create an additional place in order to do so.

13. From Moore, *Illustrated Ballad History*. Moore titles it "A Loyal Kentish Ballad."

14. The "Chevy Chase" melody, which seems, in view of the opening verse, to be the tune the author had in mind, is taken from traditional sources.

15. General Hugh Percy.

16. General Israel Putnam.

17. Major John Pitcairn of the Royal Marines and second-in-command of the British expedition to Lexington and Concord.

18. Lieutenant Colonel James Abercromby, who died of wounds after leading the grenadiers in the assaults at Bunker Hill.

19. Published in England and in Rivington's *Royal Gazette* in November 1779, according to Moore, *Songs and Ballads*.

20. The reference is to Admiral Sir Charles Hardy.

21. The "manifesto" is probably the statement delivered to the English by the French ambassador in March of 1778 announcing the conclusion of two treaties—of commerce and military alliance—between France and the United States. This led to war between France and England.

Chapter 7

1. From *Four Excellent New Songs Called "Yankee Doodle," etc.*, published in New York by John Reid, 1788. (See Bibliography.) This version, containing but twelve verses plus a chorus, has been slightly amended from the original.

2. Archaic word meaning extreme or, in this case, either long or strong.

3. From *The American Musical Miscellany* (1798).

4. The otherwise unidentified Williamson was apparently a popular variety singer whose name keeps cropping up as having sung one or another popular song in New

York, Boston or Philadelphia. An advertisement in the *Columbian Centinel* of Boston, in July 1797, lists "The Hobbies" as "a favorite song, written and sung by Mr. Williamson."

5. From many sources.

6. The composer, Philip Phile, died in 1793, five years before Hopkinson took his tune for "The President's March" and adapted it to this anthem.

7. From *The Columbian Naval Songster*, compiled by Edward Gillespy (1813).

8. The song was widely printed in broadside sheets and in songsters of the period. It is also known variously as "Hull's Victory" and "Yankee Doodle Dandy-O," although there are a number of songs celebrating the same event that go by all three titles. From Luce, *Naval Songs*. (See Bibliography.) See also Robert W. Neeser, *American Naval Songs and Ballads* (hereinafter referred to as Neeser, *American Naval Songs*), for a number of related songs.

9. From William Main Doerflinger, *Shantymen and Shantyboys*, collected from Archie Lant of New York City, who learned the ballad as a boy in Ontario.

10. From Neeser, *American Naval Songs*.

11. A traditional seaman's ballad, from Luce, *Naval Songs*. A number of ballads celebrating Perry's victory, including several others with this same title, became widely popular. For a collection of these, see Neeser, *American Naval Songs*.

12. Lieutenant John J. Yarnell (his name is misspelled in the song), a battery commander, was left in command of the *Lawrence* when Perry set out in a rowboat to take over command of the *Niagara* and so to continue the battle.

13. Lieutenant Jesse D. Elliott commanded the *Niagara*. Unlike the song, history has rendered a mixed judgment on his role in the engagement.

14. It is one of the oldest folk ballads of purely American origin. A brief historical account by Albert H. Tolman and Mary O. Eddy of the ballad and the circumstances of its creation, along with a full text and tune, appears in the *Journal of American Folklore* 35 (1922).

15. From *The United States Songster* (1836).

16. Commodore John Rodgers (his name is misspelled in the song) was the commander of the frigate *President* and served with distinction throughout the war.

17. Stephen Decatur was one of the outstanding U.S. naval commanders in the war. He was responsible for the defeat of the H.M.S. *Macedonian* on October 25, 1812 and also famous for his toast, "Our country . . . may she always be in the right, but our country, right or wrong."

18. This is a word play on the U.S.S. *Enterprise*, which beat the H.M.S. *Boxer* in a naval engagement which took place off Portland, Maine on September 5, 1813. It was a bloody action in which both the American and British captains were killed.

19. From *American Patriotic and Comic Modern Songs* (1819).

20. It was no accident that the melody chosen for Key's stirring lyrics was "To Anacreon in Heaven." The British drinking song, written about 1775, was enormously popular in America. Between 1790 and 1818 there were at least 85 parodies written which managed to find their way into print. Robert Treat Paine, Jr. used the tune for his famous "Adams and Liberty."

21. From a broadside sheet (New York Public Library). Since the action took place near the town of Plattsburg, New York, the song is sometimes known as "The Battle of Plattsburg."

22. An American commander, Lieutenant Sidney Smith, had previously (June 1813) taken two sloops, the *Growler* and the *Eagle*, up the Sorel River, which flows into Lake Champlain from the north. The British sank one and ran the other aground, later repairing them and then using them to maintain control of the lake.

23. In northeastern New York State, near Lake Champlain.

24. From Paul G. Brewster, "The Battle of New Orleans," in the *Southern Folklore Quarterly*, vol 1, no. 3 (1937). The song was sent to Brewster by Martin G. Fowler, of Petersburg, Indiana, in 1935. Fowler reported that he had learned the song from his grandfather, Thomas Fowler, "who was a captain under General Andrew Jackson, and fought in that great battle." His suggestion that the song was "composed and sung by the soldiers who fought the battle" is difficult to confirm; the burden of the evidence would seem to suggest that a communal creation is extremely doubtful. It is likely that an anonymous soldier bard in Jackson's army wrote the song.

25. The text is from a broadside sheet in the New York Public Library.

26. Helen Flanders, in *The New Green Mountain Songster*, reports that Ballou was a resident of Richmond, New Hampshire.

27. Captain William Bainbridge succeeded Isaac Hull as commander of the *Constitution* and led that ship in successful battle.

28. Captain George Downie, commander of the British fleet that was defeated by Macdonough in the Battle of Lake Champlain.

29. American forces under the command of General William Henry Harrison defeated the British troops led by General Henry A. Proctor at the Thames River in southeastern Ontario in October, 1813. The victory helped establish Harrison's military reputation and, in time, aided him in his successful presidential election campaign of 1840.

30. This is a reference to the burning by the British of the Library of Congress, along with numerous other government files and records, during their occupation of Washington in August, 1814.

Bibliography

Articles in Periodicals

Allen, Gardner W. "Naval Songs and Ballads." *Proceedings of the American Antiquarian Society*, April 1925.

Brewster, Paul G. "The Battle of New Orleans." *Southern Folklore Quarterly* 1, no. 3 (1937).

Davidson, Levette J. "Two Old War Songs." *California Folklore Quarterly* 4 (1945).

Fitch, Roscoe Conkling. "More About Yankee Doodle." *New York Times*, 24 February 1929.

Hackett, Karleton. "Notes on American Music of the XVIII Century." *Music* 21, no. 2, January 1902.

Hunt, Arthur B. "A Treasure Chest of Song from America's Dawn." *Musical America* 37, no. 14, 27 January 1923.

Newcomb, Lydia Bolles. "Songs and Ballads of the American Revolution." *New England Magazine* 13, no. 4, December 1895.

Onderdonk, James L. "Colonial Patriotism in Song." *American Historical Register* 3 (1895).

Silber, Irwin. "Scandalous Songs of 1734 Celebrated NYC Election Victory." *Sing Out!* 5, no. 3, Summer 1955.

Tolman, Albert H., and Eddy, Mary O. "Traditional Texts and Tunes." *Journal of American Folklore* 35 (1922).

General Books

Adler, Kurt. *Songs of Many Wars*. New York: Howell, Soskin & Co., 1943.

American War Songs. Philadelphia: National Committee for the Preservation of Existing Records of the National Society of the Colonial Dames of America, 1925.

Anderson, Simon V. "American Music During the War for Independence, 1775-1783." Ph.D. dissertation, University of Michigan, 1965.

Banks, Louis Albert. *Immortal Songs of Camp and Field*. Cleveland: Burrows Bros. Co., 1896.

Barney, Samuel E. *Songs of the Revolution*. New Haven: General David Humphreys Branch of the Connecticut Society of the Sons of the American Revolution, 1893.

Barry, Phillips. *British Ballads from Maine*. New Haven: Yale University Press, 1929.

Beard, Charles A. *An Economic Interpretation of the Constitution of the United States*. New York: Macmillan Co., 1913.

Brand, Oscar. *Singing Holidays*. New York: Alfred A. Knopf, 1957.

Brooks, Henry M. *Olden-Time Music*. Boston: Ticknor & Co., 1888.

Brown, Roger H. *The Republic in Peril: 1812*. New York: W. W. Norton & Co., 1971.

Buranelli, Vincent. *The Trial of Peter Zenger*. New York: New York University Press, 1957.

Chase, Gilbert. *America's Music from the Pilgrims to the Present*. New York: McGraw-Hill Book Co., 1955.

Coffin, Tristram P. *The British Traditional Ballad in North America*. Philadelphia: American Folklore Society, 1950.

Colcord, Joanna C. *Songs of American Sailormen*. New York: W. W. Norton & Co., 1938.

Damon, S. Foster. *"Yankee Doodle."* Providence, R. I.: Meriden Gravure Co., 1959.

Davidson, Philip. *Propaganda and the American Revolution, 1763-1783*. Chapel Hill: University of North Carolina Press, 1941.

Doerflinger, William Main. *Shantymen and Shantyboys*. New York: Macmillan Co., 1951.

Dolph, Edward A. *Sound Off!, Soldier Songs from Yankee Doodle to Parley Voo*. New York: Cosmopolitan Book Corp., 1929.

Downes, Olin, and Siegmeister, Elie. *A Treasury of American Song*. New York: Howell, Soskin & Co., 1940.

D'Urfey, Thomas. *Pills to Purge Melancholy*. 6 vols. 1719-20. Reprint (facsimile reproduction from the 1876 edition). New York: Folklore Library Publishers, 1959.

Eddy, Mary Olive. *Ballads and Songs from Ohio*. New York: J. J. Augustin, 1939.

Edmunds, John. *A Williamsburg Songbook*. New York: Holt, Rinehart & Winston, 1964.

Eggleston, George Cary. *American War Ballads and Lyrics*. 2 vols. New York: G. P. Putnam's Sons, 1889.

Elson, Louis C. *The History of American Music*. New York: Macmillan Co., 1904.

————. *The National Music of America*. Boston: L. C. Page & Co., 1899.

Emerick, Albert G. *Songs for the People*. Boston: Oliver Ditson Co., 1852.

Fisher, William Arms. *The Music That Washington Knew*. Boston: Oliver Ditson Co., 1931.

Fitz-Gerald, S. J. Adair. *Stories of Famous Songs*. London: John C. Nimmo, 1898.

Flanders, Helen Hartness. *The New Green Mountain Songster*. New Haven: Yale University Press, 1939.

Ford, Worthington C. *The Isaiah Thomas Collection of Ballads*. Worcester, Mass.: American Antiquarian Society, 1923.

Fowke, Edith, and Mills, Alan. *Canada's Story in Song*. Toronto: W. J. Gage, 1960.

Goldman, Richard Franko, and Smith, Roger. *Landmarks of Early American Music (1760-1800)*. New York: G. Schirmer, 1943.

Granger, Bruce Ingham. *Political Satire in the American Revolution, 1763-1783*. Ithaca, N.Y.: Cornell University Press, 1960.

Hart, Albert Bushnell. *Camps and Firesides of the Revolution*. New York: Macmillan Co., 1903.

Hastings, George Everett. *The Life and Works of Francis Hopkinson*. New York: Russell & Russell, 1926.

Haywood, Charles. *A Bibliography of North American Folksong*. New York: Greenberg Books, 1951.

Howard, John Tasker. *The Music of George Washington's Time*. Washington, D.C.: The U.S. George Washington Bicentennial Commission, 1931.

————. *Our American Music*. New York: Thomas Y. Crowell Co., 1946, 1954.

Hugill, Stan. *Shanties from the Seven Seas*. New York: E. P. Dutton & Co., 1961.

Ives, Burl. *The Burl Ives Song Book*. New York: Ballantine Books, 1953.

Jackson, G. S. *Early Songs of Uncle Sam*. Boston: B. Humphries, 1933.

James, Reese Davis. *Cradle of Culture: The Philadelphia Stage 1800-1810*. Philadelphia: University of Pennsylvania Press, 1957.

Johnson, Helen Kendrick. *Our Familiar Songs and Those Who Made Them*. New York: Henry Holt & Co., 1881.

Jordan, Philip D., and Kessler, Lillian. *Songs of Yesterday*. New York: Doubleday, Doran, 1941.

Laws, G. Malcolm. *American Balladry from British Broadsides*. Philadelphia: American Folklore Society, 1957.

————. *Native American Balladry*. Philadelphia: American Folklore Society, 1964.

Leale, Enid. *Peeps at Historical Songs*. London: A & C Black, 1927.

Loesser, Arthur. *Humor in American Song*. New York: Howell, Soskin & Co., 1942.

Lomax, Alan. *The Folk Songs of North America*. New York: Doubleday & Co., 1960.

Lossing, Benson J. *The Pictorial Field-Book of the Revolution.* 2 vols. New York: Harper & Bros., 1860.

Lowens, Irving. *Music and Musicians in Early America.* New York: W. W. Norton & Co., 1964.

Luce, S. B. *Naval Songs.* New York: William A. Pond & Co., 1908.

Marrocco, W. Thomas, and Gleason, Harold. *Music in America.* New York: W. W. Norton & Co., 1964.

Mates, Julian. *The American Musical Stage before 1800.* New Brunswick, N.J.: Rutgers University Press, 1962.

Miller, Florence Hazen. *Memorial Album of Revolutionary Soldiers, 1776.* Crete, Nebr., 1958.

Miller, John C. *Origins of the American Revolution.* Stanford, Calif.: Stanford University Press, 1959.

Moore, Frank, comp. *The Diary of the American Revolution.* Edited by John Anthony Scott. New York: Washington Square Press, 1967.

————. *Illustrated Ballad History of the American Revolution, 1765-1783.* New York: Johnson, Wilson & Co., 1876.

————. *Songs and Ballads of the American Revolution.* New York: D. Appleton & Co., 1855.

Morgan, Helen M. *A Season in New York: 1801.* Pittsburgh: University of Pittsburgh Press, 1969.

Neeser, Robert W. *American Naval Songs and Ballads.* New Haven: Yale University Press, 1938.

Odell, George C. D. *Annals of the New York Stage,* vol. 1. New York: Columbia University Press, 1927.

Patterson, Samuel White. *The Spirit of the American Revolution as Revealed in the Poetry of the Period.* Boston: Richard G. Badger, 1915.

Pichierri, Louis. *Music in New Hampshire (1623-1800).* New York: Columbia University Press, 1960.

Prescott, Frederick C., and Nelson, John H. *Prose and Poetry of the Revolution (1765-1789).* New York: Thomas Y. Crowell Co., 1925.

Randolph, Vance. *Ozark Folksongs.* 4 vols. Columbia: State Historical Society of Missouri, 1946.

Raoul, Francois Camus. "The Military Band in the United States Army Prior to 1834." Ph.D. dissertation, New York University.

Sargent, Winthrop. *The Loyalist Poetry of the Revolution.* Philadelphia, 1857.

————. *The Loyal Verses of Stanbury & Odell.* Albany, N.Y., 1860.

Savelle, Max. *The Colonial Origins of American Thought.* Princeton, N.J.: D. Van Nostrand Co., 1964.

————. *Seeds of Liberty: The Genesis of the American Mind.* Seattle: University of Washington Press, 1948.

Scheer, George F., and Rankin, Hugh F. *Rebels and Redcoats.* Cleveland: World Publishing Co., 1957.

Scott, John Anthony. *The Ballad of America: The History of the United States in Song and Story.* New York: Bantam Books, 1966.

————. *Living Documents in American History*, vol. 1. New York: Washington Square Press, 1963.

Sharp, Cecil J. *English Folk Songs from the Southern Appalachians*. 2 vols. London: Oxford University Press, 1932.

Silber, Irwin. *Songs America Voted By*. Harrisburg, Pa.: Stackpole Co., 1971.

Simpson, Claude M. *The British Broadside Ballad and Its Music*. New Brunswick, N.J.: Rutgers University Press, 1966.

Sonneck, Oscar G. *A Bibliography of Early Secular American Music (18th Century)*. Revised by William Treat Upton. New York: DaCapo Press, 1964.

————. *Early Concert Life in America (1731-1800)*. New York: Musurgia Publishers, 1949.

————. *Report on "The Star Spangled Banner," "Hail Columbia," "America" and "Yankee Doodle."* Washington, D.C.: Government Printing Office for the Library of Congress, 1909.

Stone, William L. *Ballads and Poems Relating to the Burgoyne Campaign*. Albany, N.Y.: Joel Munsell's Sons, 1893.

Thompson, Harold W. *Body, Boots & Britches*. Philadelphia: J.B. Lippincott Co., 1940.

Tucker, Glenn. *Poltroons and Patriots: A Popular Account of the War of 1812*. Indianapolis: Bobbs-Merrill Co., 1954.

Tyler, Moses Coit. *Literary History of the American Revolution*. New York: Knickerbocker Press, 1897.

Vernon, Grenville. *Yankee Doodle-Doo: A Collection of Songs of the Early American Stage*. New York: Payson & Clarke, 1927.

White, Newman Ivey. *The Frank C. Brown Collection of North Carolina Folklore*. 5 vols. Durham, N.C.: Duke University Press, 1952-60.

Winslow, Ola Elizabeth. *American Broadside Verse from Imprints of the 17th and 18th Centuries*. New Haven: Yale University Press, 1930.

Winstock, Lewis. *Songs and Music of the Redcoats: A History of the War Music of the British Army, 1642-1902*. Harrisburg, Pa.: Stackpole Co., 1970.

Wolfe, Richard J. *Secular Music in America, 1801-1825: A Bibliography*. 3 vols. New York: New York Public Library, 1964.

Period Songsters

Aeolian Harp and Singer's Nonpareil, The. New York: G. W. & S. Turney, n.d.

American Minstrel, The. Cincinnati: J. A. James & Co., 1836.

American Musical Miscellany, The. Northampton, Mass.: Daniel Wright & Co., 1798.

American Patriotic and Comic Modern Songs. New York: John Low, 1819.

American Patriotic Song Book, The. Philadelphia: John Bioren, 1816.

American Songster, The. Compiled by John Kenedy. Baltimore: John Kenedy, 1836.

American Songster, The. New York: Samuel Campbell, 1788.

BIBLIOGRAPHY

Baltimore Musical Miscellany or Columbian Songster, The. 2 vols. Baltimore: S. Butler, 1805.

Bay Psalm Book. Boston, 1698.

Boston Musical Miscellany, The. Boston: J. T. Buckingham, 1811.

Buck's Pocket Companion or Merry Fellow, The. New York: Lazarus Beach, 1803.

Collection of the Newest Cotillions and Country Dances, A. Worcester, Mass., 1800.

Columbian Harmonist, The. Philadelphia: Thomas Simpson, 1814.

Columbian Naval Melody, The. Boston, 1813.

Columbian Naval Songster, The. Compiled and arranged by Edward Gillespy. New York, 1813.

Comic Songs. Philadelphia, 1814.

Democratic Songster, The. Baltimore: Keating's Book Store, 1794.

Eagle and Harp. Baltimore, 1812.

Father Kemp's Old Folks' Concert Tunes. Revised and enlarged edition. Boston: Oliver Ditson Co., 1889.

Federal Songster, The. New London, Conn.: James Springer, 1800.

Festival of Mirth and American Tar's Delight, The. New York: Thomas B. Jansen & Co., 1800.

Forecastle Songs & Yarns (Jack's Kit: or Saturday Night in the Forecastle . . . by an Old Salt). New York, n.d.

Four Excellent New Songs Called "Yankee Doodle," "Death of General Wolfe," "Nancy Dawson," "Guardian Angels." New York: John Reid, 1788.

Household Songbook, The. New York: Leavitt & Allen, ca. 1830.

Humming Bird, The. Boston, 1798.

Hymen's Recruiting Sergeant: or the New Matrimonial Tat-too, for the Old Bachelors. Greenfield, Mass., 1817.

Masonick Minstrel, The. Dedham, Mass., 1816.

New England Psalm-Singer or American Chorister, The. Boston: Edes and Gill, 1770.

New National Songbook, The. New York: Leavitt & Allen, 1856.

Nightingale of Liberty or Delights of Harmony, The. New York: John Harrison, 1797.

Nightingale, or Musical Companion, The. New York: Smith & Forman, 1814.

Patriotick and Amatory Songster, The. Boston: Samuel Avery, 1810.

Philadelphia Songster, Part I, The. Compiled by Absalom Aimwell. Philadelphia: John McCulloch, 1789.

Political Songster, The. Birmingham, England: John Free, 1784.

Poor Man's Advice to His Poor Neighbors: A Ballad to the Tune of "Chevy-Chace," The. New York, 1774.

Skylark, or Gentleman and Ladies Complete Songster, The. Worcester, Mass.: Isaiah Thomas, 1795.

Soldier's Companion, The. New York: Leavitt & Allen, 1856.

Song-Singer's Amusing Companion, The. Boston: Sterne and Mann, 1818.

Songs of the Revolution; Songs of the Late War, Naval and Military Victories, and Patriotic Odes. New York: Wilson & Co., 1844.

Songster's Museum, The. Hartford, Conn.: Henry Benton, 1829.

Star-Spangled Banner, The. Wilmington, Del.: J. Wilson, 1816.

Tilden's Miscellaneous Poems on Diverse Occasions. Printed in 1756.

United States Songster, The. Cincinnati: U. P. James, 1836.

Vocal Miscellany, The. London: J. & J. Hazard, 1738.

Phonograph Records

American Revolution, The, by Richard Bales, a cantata based on the music of the American Colonies during the years 1775-1800. Performed by the Cantata Choir of the Lutheran Church of the Reformation and the National Gallery Orchestra. Columbia Records LL-1001.

American Revolution Through Its Songs and Ballads, The. Sung and narrated by Bill Bonyun, J. Anthony Scott and Gene Bonyun. Heirloom Records HL-502.

Ballads of the American Revolution and the War of 1812. Sung by John and Lucy Allison and Sawyer's Minutemen. RCA-VICTOR VI-P11.

Ballads of the Revolution. Sung by Wallace House. Folkways Records FH-5001.

Ballads of the War of 1812. Sung by Wallace House. Folkways Records FH-5002.

Bay State Ballads. Sung by Paul Clayton. Folkways Records FP-47/2.

Champlain Valley Songs. Sung by Pete Seeger. Folkways Records FH-5210.

Folksongs from Martha's Vineyard. Sung by E. G. Huntington. Folkways Records FA-2032.

War Ballads, U.S.A. Sung by Hermes Nye. Folkways Records FH-5249.

Index of Tunes

Songs with words set to well-known tunes may be found on the pages indicated below. Songs whose titles are printed in italics are accompanied by the music. All others have the words only.

Index of Song Titles

(* indicates both words and music)

Index of Persons, Places, and Events